Three Tests for Democracy

STUDIES IN PHILOSOPHY

CONSULTING EDITOR / V. C. CHAPPELL
THE UNIVERSITY OF CHICAGO

DAVID BRAYBROOKE

Dalhousie University

Three Tests for Democracy /
Personal Rights,
Human Welfare,
Collective Preference

RANDOM HOUSE New York

TO MY MOTHER AND FATHER:
my first audience—
still appreciative; still critical

Contents

Three Tests for Democracy

PROLOGUE

Many people have advocated democracy—some of them famous and articulate, most of them obscure and unskilled in speech. Almost everybody in every English-speaking country reckons himself an advocate; so do common and uncommon men in many other countries. Advocating democracy, people usually indicate that they want a certain sort of government for themselves. They may believe that they already have such a government; they may believe that they can obtain one only by revolutionary action. In either case they claim the support as needed of democrats in other countries; and themselves support the progress of democracy elsewhere. Taking up a position as an advocate of democracy amounts, then, to announcing some readiness for an active role in politics, though the role envisaged may not be a leading one, or even active enough to be dangerous.

To direct their actions rationally, so that the actions make for democracy rather than for something else, advocates must be able to discriminate between governments good in their eyes and governments not so good. They discriminate by means of concepts—the concepts that they would draw upon to explain how what democrats advocate in the way of government differs from the governments their opponents might contend for. To apply any of these concepts to a government means subjecting the government to a certain test, which it may pass or fail, or satisfy in various degrees. As a result of making such tests, advocates of democracy pass judgment on the governments (or possible governments) that they have considered. These judgments complete a process of evaluation, conducted on lines distinctive of advocates of democracy, at least when these lines combine.

Evaluation prepares the way for action and derives its interest from the connection. This book, however, assumes that evaluation is a process itself needing attention. The book will concentrate upon explicating some features of the approach to evaluation that democratic thinking inspires. I shall ask what sorts of tests do the concepts of personal rights, human welfare, and collective preference bring to bear upon governments? These are prominent among the concepts advanced by advocates of democracy. They are not, of course, the only concepts so advanced. Taken together, they suffice to give a fairly comprehensive account of what democrats look for in passing judgment upon governments; but other accounts, differently shaped because they would be built around different concepts, might have at least equally good claims to being comprehensive. Such concepts, to which I shall give relatively little attention in this book, include the concepts of liberty, social justice, equality. I choose to concentrate upon rights, welfare, and collective preference because I think these concepts have been less adequately explicated than some others in the democratic tool box; and hence are in worse need of attempts at philosophical investigation.

If evaluation issues in action, people will naturally seek to safeguard themselves against misguided actions by taking precautions against mistaken evaluations—mistaken either in the ways given tests are carried out or fundamentally misguided in not carrying out the right tests. In traditional discussions political philosophy has given the place of honor to the question,

"Are these the right tests?" I am going to discuss the concepts of rights, welfare, and collective preference at some length; but I am not going to deal, except incidentally, with the question "Are these at bottom the right tests?" or the question "Are we justified in using them to evaluate governments?" I say this without belittling such questions; and without belittling other questions in political philosophy that I am not going to discuss either, such as questions about sovereignty, or authority, or political obligation. I am not going to defend the legitimacy of democracy as a form of government. I am going to explain (in part) what advocates of democracy demand of governments before they will judge them acceptable.

My explanation, it is true, will go somewhat beyond describing what advocates of democracy are now demanding. I shall (especially in my treatment of rights and collective preference) supply constructions to fill gaps between what advocates are now demanding and the measure of explicit content required for tests relevant to contemporary governments with contemporary problems. If anyone wished to, he might insist that these constructions amounted to recommendations that the concepts be developed in such ways. But if they are recommendations, they still serve my chief aim, which is to explicate those concepts in their present state. For the constructions will be designed to depart only incrementally from what usage has already established as features of the concepts; and to go no further in developing other features than present users might be expected to consent to, once they saw the intellectual need for formulating definite contemporary tests to apply the concepts. By working within these limits I may hope to indicate what the limits are, and hence fill out my description of the present state of the concepts, a state that includes tendencies toward development in some directions rather than others.

There is at least one effect of many inquiries into the foundations of democracy that I hope this book will help remedy even though it does not itself discuss foundations. The inconclusive confusion in which those inquiries have all too often lapsed has, I think, given the impression that there is something inadequate in the concepts that justification and foundations were sought for. Are they not too vague and elusive to support significant tests of government? But difficulty in finding foundations does not at all imply difficulty, much less impossibility, in using the concepts themselves. I hope to show that the concepts of personal rights, human welfare, and collective preference all furnish clear and intelligible tests, often very simple and straightforward ones; though perhaps it will turn out that the concepts which the reader begins by thinking clearest among these three do not remain clearest under close examination.

I shall put forward a number of theses about the meaning of the concepts of personal rights, human welfare, and collective preference. They will be simultaneously theses about tests of government that involve those concepts. Some of the theses will be very risky ones, for which I can supply neither adequate evidence nor adequate arguments. I put them forward anyway, in the hope that my intuition has led me to useful points of departure for later discussion and correction.

All of the theses risk being upset by evidence spontaneously offered by advocates of democracy. In their daily use of the terms that I try to explicate they make their own disclosures about the implications with which they use the terms. My theses go beyond this spontaneous evidence to presume on what advocates of democracy would say in response to questioning about these implications, once they had heard some argument. By this presumption I extend the range of observations relevant to confirming or disconfirming my explications; I do not put my theses out of observational reach. Indeed, I have myself made some observations in the further range, though, characteristically, as a philosopher I have made them in the course of practicing dialectic rather than by conducting anything like a survey of opinion.

Would surveys be irrelevant? I mean by "advocates of democracy" primarily real people, alive today, ordinary men and women with some experience of politics in the English-speaking countries, who consciously favor their governments because they believe the governments have democratic features. I suppose that they have had classes in civics at school and some practice in carrying on the business of clubs and other voluntary organizations as well as a history of participating in elections. Some of them may have read the principal documents of our political tradition, including the works of philosophers like Locke; and on this basis some of them may be very articulate about their beliefs in democracy.

My theses concern how these real people use certain terms of ordinary language and what they would agree on as accurately describing the implications with which they use them. I do not think that a survey collecting their answers to questions about usage would be irrelevant. Even a superficial survey with a list of primitive questions might help to fix the size and membership of the linguistic community to which my remarks apply. Perhaps my intuitions about usage extend (on the points crucial to my present theses) only to a small class of other people, philosophers trained like myself by professors of the British analytical school. A survey of these philosophers might show that I am mistaken even about them.

On the other hand, I can in fact communicate on the subject of rights not only with other philosophers but with anyone who can competently speak my language. Putting aside slips of tongue and pen there are all sorts of gross errors about usage that I am pretty safe from making, as a user myself. I am not, for example, very liable to confuse the meanings of the terms "right," "rite," and "wright," even when they are all preceded by an article. To test my theses about implications, I expect a survey would have to search beyond the level of such gross errors. Since the theses concern what people—advocates of democracy —would agree to after dialectic, the survey would have to incorporate adequate provisions for dialectic; unfortunately, it would then probably be too protracted and expensive to carry out.

I have tested most of the theses of the present book by practicing dialectic upon them: I have offered them in various versions to other speakers of my language, who have putatively shared my usage of the terms in question, and I have modified the theses to accommodate their objections and counterexamples. Before I wrote out extended arguments about the theses, I tried out many related ideas piecemeal in discussions with university students (a much more representative sample of advocates of democracy than samples consisting merely of professors). After I had written out extended arguments, I then took the opportunity to propound them to various audiences and to collect the objections of professors, my colleagues. Hence, although my theses do not issue from a systematic survey, a lot of dialectic has gone into them. Ironically, the least has gone into the theses at the end of the book, my final theses on collective preference, which are perhaps more daring than any of the others; my discussion there developed too late to be given the tryouts that the rest of the book has had.

All my theses, however, not just these, are offered the reader subject to improvement by further dialectic. I invite the reader to engage in that dialectic, hoping that he will not be content with refuting what I say, but will try to preserve whatever parts of the truth I may have come on, pruning away my mistakes, and adding insights of his own. I suppose that the readers of this book will almost inevitably be advocates of democracy themselves, Western liberal democrats like me. They should compare what I say they think with what they themselves think they say.

*A*dvocates of democracy have made much use of the concept of *rights* in evaluating governments. Particular rights function as so many particular social devices, the primary purpose of which is to regulate human interaction in organized society, and to regulate this interaction on behalf of various identified or identifiable persons. But given the existence of such devices, they and others brought forward under the same concept readily lend themselves to a secondary use, in which a government's policies regarding rights is made a test for distinguishing good governments from bad ones. Governments that respect and maintain rights are so far as this test carries weight good governments. Governments that violate rights or fail to uphold them are thus far bad governments.

Use of the test of rights does not by itself signify the presence of anything like a full array of democratic beliefs. *Magna Carta* is a document inspired through and through by a concern for rights (or for "liberties," where we would now speak of rights); but *Magna Carta* is not a democratic document. It ascribes rights to all men in England, not merely to barons, as cursory allusions to it too often imply: merchants and villeins are included as well as lords and bishops. It calls upon the King to refrain from tampering with any of the rights that it enumerates, whoever they are ascribed to. But the rights enumerated vary greatly between different sorts of men; heeding them is quite compatible with maintaining a strict hierarchy of social roles, which subordinate some sorts of men to others without recourse or remission. The King must not tamper with rights, because doing so undermines the foundations of society; but no provision is made for the people to tamper with them either, whether to extend their scope or to increase the proportions of people holding one right or another. The rights are fixed, and feudal society is entrenched behind them.

One reason why present-day democrats make use of the test of rights is historical: it was by means of certain innovations in application of the concept of rights that considerations specifically important to democracy were first and most effectively publicized. The vitality of the concept of rights, however, does not arise from this precedent alone; but from other sources besides. The concept is one of the most prominent and popular features of ordinary moral discourse, in daily use by all sorts of people in all sorts of matters of great personal concern to them. Moreover, the concept is by design peculiarly stringent and individualistic, which makes it a debating weapon fascinating in potency for one's own side, and too dangerous to leave for preemption by others. Democratic thinkers would have plenty of reasons for using the concept of rights even if their predecessors had not made so much of it.

1 / The Concept
of Rights Analyzed

1.1. Perfectionism and Individualism

The stringency of the concept of personal rights goes hand in hand with its peculiarly emphatic individualism. Other concepts used by democrats are individualistic, too: it is a failing on the part of a government to neglect the welfare of any individual person; it is also a failing to ignore his preferences about public policy (even when it is not a failing to deviate from them). Yet a government could excuse itself at least for the first failing by demonstrating, first, that it had provided for the welfare of a number of other people, and had met the preferences of a number; and, second, that its resources and circumstances were such that it could hardly have served greater numbers, and hence done better in either respect.

Rights may be invented and maintained as means of promoting welfare. Often a test of governmental performance in respect to rights will amount indirectly to a test in respect to welfare. But welfare may be investigated directly. When this happens, and when the objects of comparison are governments acknowledged to be incapable of perfect performances because of limited resources, the test of performance in respect to welfare will turn upon comparisons of statistics about the proportions of populations whose welfare has been provided for. Similarly, in comparisons of imperfect governments in respect to collective preference, the evidence crucial to ordinary tests will be evidence about proportions of people expressing preferences and the extent to which policies are suited to these proportions. These concepts are used without presupposing that any government can with ordinary care entirely escape failings in individual cases. It is commonplace knowledge that resources are often insufficient. It is also commonplace knowledge that people's preferences are liable to conflict radically, so no government can be expected to satisfy all of them simultaneously.

A perfectionist presupposition does accompany the concept of rights. Admittedly, rough comparisons between imperfect governments may sometimes be made plausible; one government (though failing to respect all rights or the rights of all persons) may be found to do more to respect rights than another. But according to the presupposition, doing better, if it is less than doing perfectly well, must still be judged a needless failure. A government without the available resources to provide for everybody's welfare and not subtle enough to reconcile all conflicts of preferences can nevertheless, with ordinary care, and apart from extraordinary emergencies, do everything required to respect everyone's rights. What it has to do, to respect them, is simply to refrain from doing anything to violate them. Every observed violation, however few people affected—perhaps only one man—is an immediate occasion for protest.

Maintaining rights by active intervention is another matter. It is essential, for a government to meet this side of the test of rights, that rights be consistent with one another; it is essential also that the government have sufficient means—for example, a sufficiently large and efficient police force. These requirements may by common acknowledgment be out of reach in some circumstances; hence individualism cannot be carried to a perfectionist extreme on this side of the test of rights. Yet, even on this side, rights are by intention nonconflicting—inconsistencies that defeat the purpose of maintaining every right for every person arise only because of confusion and ignorance in formulating the rights and the prescriptions they entail. Furthermore, the maintenance of rights is in the eyes of leading democratic thinkers so much the first minimum business of government that a government without the means to maintain them would hardly in their eyes have begun to function. If government is—normally —practical, the maintenance of rights must—normally —be practical too.

Individualistic in application, the concept of rights is also individualistic in administration. There are, of course, social agencies that assist in the administration of rights—the police and the courts, for example—just as there are social agencies for undertaking other tasks of government. A good part of the administration of rights, however, is left to the individual persons who have them and who, having them, must decide whether or not to exercise them and when.

Rights encourage individual self-reliance in one's own defense. Every man—or, at least, every man and his lawyer—is his own administrator, capable and responsible under the concept of initiating defensive action against other people—private persons or official ones. Thus a man, invoking his rights, defends his privacy; recovers his property; obtains the use of public facilities. Every man is likewise capable of being his own evaluator, putting the concept of rights to its secondary use of evaluating governments, by beginning with his own case. How, he may ask, does the government do in respect to *my* rights? If it disregards any of them it is thus far to be judged bad, never mind how it treats other people's rights. For attending to other people's rights is no excuse for ignoring *mine*.

The concept of rights offers advocates of democracy the means of awakening widespread personal interest and popular activity. But how are these means to be used? Not every particular right equally suits democratic purposes in evaluation and advocacy; some rights presuppose feudalism, or another form of hierarchical social organization. The democrat must choose, from a mixed bag of endlessly varying formulations, the rights that he can make best use of. Before he chooses, however, it will be well for him to become clearer about the concept of rights itself. Just what are rights that so much is made of them?

1.2. Rules Corresponding to Rights

Two-part Rules: Exercise and Status. To say that a person, N, "has a right to *x*" or that he "has a right to do *a*" (which is more fundamental) is in both cases logically equivalent to setting forth a complex rule, which includes two propositions to the effect (1) that if N does a certain action or actions, then M, some other person or persons fulfilling certain conditions, are called upon to do or refrain from doing a certain other action or actions and (2) that the fact just set forth implies a certain status for N, vis-à-vis M, and perhaps vis-à-vis other people as well, not to be classed with M, which even should N fail to do any of the actions first mentioned requires M, and perhaps these other people, to do some actions and refrain from doing others. (The expressions "setting forth" and "called upon" will be explained together later. I shall then also qualify my use of "proposition.")

Proposition (1) expresses the *exercisable* aspect of a right; Proposition (2) expresses the *status* aspect. The existence of N's right in its status aspect is a necessary condition of the existence of his right in its exercisable aspect. Some discussions of rights neglect the status aspect to such an extent as to suggest that a right may be ignored when the person holding the right omits to exercise it. But having a right typically requires other people to do or refrain from doing various things whether or not the person holding the right exercises it, invokes it, thinks about it, or knows of its existence. If N has a right to certain movable items of property, the items are not to be appropriated by other people even if N is not using them himself. Similarly, if a person has a right to free speech, other people are not to interfere with his opportunities for free speech, even if there is no prospect of N in fact making use of any of these opportunities. Moreover, in both these cases, other people may be required to render concrete assistance toward the protection of N's status.

N's status (as an aspect of a given right) may, in the case of some rights, be accorded him without his having to do anything to earn it. He may have the status accorded him because he has inherited a certain social position; or because he is a member of a certain social class; or just because he is a fellow citizen; or just because he is a human being. In the case of some rights, the status may be something that everyone—or at least some people—must earn or otherwise qualify for by performing some previous action: by N's doing work for M, or work on his own account; by N's paying over money to M. N's right to a specific item of private property may derive from either class of rights—as being, for example, inherited, or as being earned. The status associated with this right, whether earned or unearned, is susceptible to being extinguished, and with it the right, sometimes without N's voluntary participation, and perhaps even without compensating him for its extinction (as when it is removed by court order in order to pay a fine).

Rights are generalizable. Conceivably, "N" in the rule might stand for one historic person who had by grant of his sovereign or his fellow-citizens been accorded a unique right, never given to anyone else. One might imagine "M" standing for other historic persons uniquely concerned with heeding the rule: the persons who must open the gate when N comes to enjoy his freedom of the sacred precincts. Generally speaking, however, "N" and "M" stand for any members of classes of persons—classes renewed and enlarged by the change of generations and succession of different persons to similar social roles. Anyone with such-and-such status will have the right; anyone who fulfills such-and-such conditions is called upon to do or to refrain: to depart from N's house, to return his property, to leave him alone; to help him defend himself.

Third Part Added to Rules: Conditions for Status. The conditions, such as they may be, surrounding the status referred to in part (2), are perhaps best formulated by adding a third part to the expression of the rule: Proposition (3), to the effect that N's having the status referred to in Proposition (2) implies (in its turn) the fulfillment of various conditions by N and other people, conditions which together are both necessary and sufficient for N's being accorded the relevant status.

These conditions, which would be spelled out when

the rule for a given right was spelled out, vary enormously from one right to another. In some cases the conditions would very easily, even automatically, be fulfilled, without action on N's part or anybody else's; in other cases only by a concatenation of contingencies, each requiring the consent and action of various people. Any person N failing to fulfill the conditions would fail, of course, to have the status; and if he did not have the status, he would not hold the right in its exercisable aspect either. Whether N's right contingently originated in a grant from other people, and whether—contingently originating in this way or not—the right was extinguishable, and by whom, would be shown by spelling out the conditions mentioned in Proposition (3) of the corresponding rule. Similarly, Proposition (3), fully formulated, would show whether or not, and by what procedures, if such procedures were available, N could alienate the right.

The right to a specific item of private property is an example, indeed the leading example, of an alienable right. The status connected with it, attained in various ways, can be given up, and when this is given up, the exercisable aspect of the right disappears. Attaining the status implies that the item in question was acquired by finding, or earning, or purchase, or by gift or inheritance; continuing to have the status implies that the item has not been sold or given away, or forfeited.

Inalienable Rights. Are there any *inalienable* rights? Pretty clearly there are; and since these are (so far as I can see) also rights that cannot be extinguished, the traditional extension of "inalienable" to cover what would otherwise have to be called the "inextinguishable" feature of certain rights can be decently excused.

Some rights are "inalienable" because it would not

make sense for anyone to give them up—any attempt to do so would be logically ineffective. They are "inextinguishable" because no procedure exists whereby other people could cancel them.

Indeed, it is *typical* of rights that they cannot properly be abridged without the consent, or at least the legislative participation, of the person or persons holding the rights. Rights that exist only on the sufferance of the people who have granted them are exceptional and degenerate cases. Even in those cases, to say, "N has a right to *x*," or "N has a right to do *a*," means more than that it would not be wrong for N to do certain things; for now servants and policemen and neighbors, for example, are called on to respect successful exercise and to assist in protecting N against undue interference. N, for his part, has certain expectations on which he can base definite plans; the others for their part concede the legitimacy of the expectations.

Some rights cannot be abridged even with N's consent. Consider the right to a fair trial (in the United States, the larger right to due process of law); or the right to free speech. A man of an especially servile or masochistic disposition might perhaps on some occasion feel ready to say, "I renounce my right to a fair trial" or "I hereby give up my right to free speech." But what sense would there be in his saying either of these things?

His saying them would make no more sense than your saying or my saying, "I declare the currency of the United States worthless" or "I declare Nova Scotia to be French-speaking." There are some things that we can do by words: appoint somebody to take our place for certain purposes; agree in our own person to buy a house; renounce citizenship in a particular country. Such verbal performances change the world; but

their scope is understood to be defined by prior provisions for correct procedures and suitable occasions.
Without such acknowledged provisions the performances would be logically out of place. They are out of
place in the case of inalienable rights. No person, on
any occasion, ever has the acknowledged power necessary to give up his right to a fair trial or his right to
free speech. To attempt to do so betrays a miscon-
ception of what these rights amount to, as we understand them.

By emigrating to Haiti or some other charming
country, an especially servile or masochistic person
might put himself in the hands of people who could
be counted on to infringe his right to a fair trial
or to free speech. Likewise, a government might, by
decree or by some form of legislation, instruct its
minions to hold bloody assizes rather than fair trials
and to suppress free speech rather than protect free
speakers. But this is similarly beside the point. As the
rights to a fair trial and to free speech are understood
by people using our language, no government has or
could have the acknowledged power necessary to
abolish those rights. Any laws or decrees purporting
to extinguish these rights would be logically *ultra
vires* and hence void.

Rights that people have put beyond the powers of
government to extinguish are rights that they have put
beyond their own powers, too, whether to extinguish
or to alienate. Historically, they have regarded these
rights as somehow implicit in the nature of man and
of human society; or they have regarded the rights as
conferred on men by God. The latter position, looking
to Divine authority and decree, begs fewer questions
about confusing moral notions with descriptive ones,
though it has the weakness of depending on religious
belief. Even the former position may well attract some

conviction, however; for it may be argued that unless various rights are maintained, human society will not work, or will not have certain widely desired properties. I shall not argue for either position; or for combining them. Such doctrines may in the past have led advocates of democracy to understand certain rights as inalienable—beyond even their own powers to alienate or extinguish; but this understanding may perfectly well survive abandoning the doctrines. It survives so long as no procedures are accepted, or even imagined, for alienating or extinguishing certain rights. I shall later discuss reasons for thinking that understanding various rights in this way, far from being misguided, continues to be useful, at least within limits.

1.3. Rules for Rights Distinguished from Other Rules

Many (though not all) of the rules that define social activities and the roles that people play in them concern relations between different persons and reciprocal actions (or inactions). When one person does certain actions, he looks to others to respond by doing appropriate actions of their own, or at least by refraining from doing inappropriate ones. Are these other people, then, always being "called upon" in the same sense as the people called upon by setting forth a rule under the concept of rights? The time has come to consider the notion of calling upon more carefully; once we have done so, we shall be in a position to clear up the notion of setting forth, too.

Consider the following cases: (1) N is a concert-goer, M a member of the orchestra, indeed the first trumpeter. N may expect M to play the right note in a certain passage of the overture; he has paid for his ticket and come to hear the music correctly played. Does he have a right to have M play the right note? (2) N is another player in the orchestra, say the percussionist; his sounding a drum tap gives M the cue to play a certain flourish on the trumpet. Does N have a right to have M play this flourish, once the cue has been given? Here, as in the first case, M is surely called upon to play as expected; and here the calling upon is directly signified by an action of N's. (3) N, a sergeant, orders a platoon, to which M belongs, to present arms. M may fail to do so. Does N, who by his command has certainly and quite explicitly called upon M to present arms, have a right to have M do so? (4) Two men pick up baseball gloves, and one of them, N, a ball; they separate to a distance of forty feet and face one another; N then throws the ball to the other man, M. M is called upon to catch it (if he can) and (at any rate) to throw it back. If he steps aside, however, has any right of N's been violated? (5) N sets himself up on a street corner to hawk windup toys to passersby. As his spiel begins, a small audience gathers. The people in the audience, who include M, are certainly being called on to buy the toys. Does the hawker have a right that requires M or anyone else in the audience to respond? (6) N and M are introduced to one another. N offers M his hand. Does he have a right to a handshake? (7) N and M know each other and have hitherto not been on hostile terms. N encounters M on the street and greets him. Can M snub him without violating one of his rights?

In all of these cases, N acts so as to establish a context of action, in which a reciprocal action is called for and may reasonably be expected to occur, as everyone participating in the context understands. Yet I hold that the callings upon in none of these cases have the sense of rights. In some cases, I suggest, they fail to have the sense of rights because N cannot compel M to reciprocate; nor will other people help to compel M. Compulsion does not enter the picture. Clearly it does not in the streethawker's case; I hold that it does not, in any relevant strength, in the pitch-and-catch case, either, or the cases in which M may spurn N's hand or fail to acknowledge his greeting. In these cases, N and onlookers may reproach M for his disappointing behavior. When it is clear that M really does not want to play pitch-and-catch, however, the reproaches will normally end. M's discourtesies regarding the handshake and the greeting may be taken more seriously; in some special contexts N and other people may follow them up by forcing M to apologize. I am not sure that something like a right does not begin to be visible then, though the language of rights may not be used. Normally, however, M's discourtesies will not be systematically followed up. He may have lost a possible friend or two in consequence; but he will not be compelled to shake hands or return N's greeting, or compensate N for having omitted to do these things.

If M plays the wrong note, it may be that he could not help doing so; if he is an able and conscientious trumpeter otherwise, no question of punishment may arise, and neither N nor anyone else (including M's employer) has a right that has been violated. If M deliberately plays the wrong note, however, compulsion enters the picture; the management will not keep a player who deliberately ruins a performance. Likewise, compulsion enters relevantly into the other orchestral case; and into the military example. In the orchestral cases, however, N does not have a right that M violates if M fails to respond. The compulsion will not be exerted to enforce a right of N's (though he may benefit), but to enforce a right of management's;

the option of invoking compulsion lies with the management, not with N.

The military example requires subtler treatment. It shows that we cannot simply say rights are distinguished by being backed with systematic compulsion, even though—as the other examples show—many callings upon differ from the callings upon associated with rights in not being so backed. In the military example, a great deal—perhaps a maximum—of systematic compulsion is present. If M fails to present arms, to be sure, he is defying discipline—the organizational hierarchy of the army, not just the particular sergeant confronting him; but he is defying N, the sergeant, too, and N may invoke compulsion. We cannot say that the sergeant does not have a right in the matter because superiors do not have rights in relation to inferiors; for though this comment has some value, it is not strictly true: parents have rights in relation to their children, even while these are inferior in strength. Does N, the sergeant, have no right because he has no option? He cannot let M's defiance pass. If the platoon commander is watching, he will not let N let it pass. But though rights typically are optional in respect to exercise, not all rights are; people do not have an option about exercising their right to a fair trial.

I suggest that the reason why we do not normally or naturally speak of a "right" in the sergeant's case is that we cannot easily imagine anyone's interfering with the sergeant from outside. Assuming that N's command, "Present arms!" is not itself an act of disobedience, the whole army—a formidable self-enclosed bureaucracy—backs N in the execution of his duties and in the maintenance of discipline. Suppose, however, that some conflict arises between the military and civil authorities. N and his platoon have been sent to garrison a small town and the civil authorities there try to prevent him from giving an order. Then, I think, we would begin to speak of N's right to give the command, "Present arms!" and other commands; and simultaneously imply that compulsion outside the normal military routine might legitimately be employed to enforce N's right.

So extended, I think the military example throws light on how rights first come to be spoken of when they are added to practices already established and familiar. It also throws light on the general relation of rights to compulsion. We speak of a right, I suggest, only when there is (or has been) a real prospect of N's being obstructed by other people in doing whatever the rights entitle him to—which is typically something quite definitely circumscribed. According N various rights amounts to according him, piecemeal, in various particular connections where there is (or has been) a genuine need on his part for such devices, the means of invoking systematic compulsion against people otherwise expectably equal or superior in power. Where comprehensive social provisions for superordination and subordination exist, as in military discipline, N normally has no need for the piecemeal help of such devices, when he is acting on the authority conferred upon him by these other provisions.

The callings upon associated with rights differ, then, from many other callings upon by being connected (as they are not) with systematic compulsion exertable on behalf of the possessor of the right, for his benefit or (as with a parent) in execution of his functions. They differ from other callings upon, which are connected with systematic compulsion, in not having the support of a comprehensive system of superordination and subordination among agents, which would make piecemeal devices for invoking compulsion superfluous. Whether the compulsion will actually be exerted or not depends typically (though not always) on the possessor's initiative in exercising his right, and in calling for enforcement if the exercise runs into interference. More precisely, to say that N has a right implies that the right is or ought to be enforceable by systematic compulsion if compulsion of this sort would be effective in cases of this kind.

The means of invoking systematic compulsion contemplated in assertions of rights are legal means; and the implied systematic nature of the compulsion behind rights is the systematic nature of ordinary legal processes. Either the compulsion is now available in the law or it ought to be. The callings upon associated with rights are further distinguishable from other callings upon by their complex relationship to the law and to moral endorsement.

This complex relationship consists in rights and their callings upon being subject to a double variation. A right and thus its callings upon may or may not be morally endorsed; and they are either asserted as already matters of law or championed as deserving recognition with the force of law.

Of the four possible joint cases that result from this double variation, only three require to be considered. A right championed as an addition to the law without being morally endorsed would awaken at most only technical interest; if any substantial benefits or drawbacks hung upon it, the question of moral endorsement would stand in the way, and have to be entered, before the addition could be rationally approved. The three important cases of the double variation all concern either moral endorsement or an assertion of fact about present law or both together; and the case of both together, the paradigm of rights, overshadows the other two.

When a right no longer commands moral endorsement it either becomes a dead letter or its exercise begins to invite disputation. Why should it be exercised or respected if it no longer has moral backing? On the other hand, a right that has not yet entered into law invites disputation by coming forward as a proposal—legal-in-intention, demanding assessment on both moral and legal grounds before it becomes legal-in-fact. By contrast, a right that has both moral endorsement and legal recognition has (at least for the time being) settled in place: it is fully a right, with no questions shaking it.

I hold that saying N has a certain right is logically equivalent to setting forth a complex rule, consisting of propositions about various matters, including callings upon. Now, I think that generally speaking what rights-formulas express—declarations of rights—do have truth-values; so that it is reasonable to hold they are equivalent to propositions, which as such must be true or false. Declarations of inalienable rights, I think, always have a truth-value. If they have not been made matters of law, such rights are championed not merely as deserving to be created legally, at the discretion of the people addressed, but as demanding suitable arrangements for enforcement not yet provided.

In less important cases, a declaration of right may not have a truth-value on certain occasions: when, for example, it appears in a bill proposing the enactment of just that right, or in a promulgation granting the right for the first time, or in an official statute book, the declaration is not true (or false), though its appearance then makes the declaration on other occasions true. The equivalent rule would not have a truth-value on the occasions that the declaration did not; and one should strictly speaking refrain (on those occasions) from calling its chief components "propositions."

Setting forth in these instances would amount to performing one stage or another of the process of formally enacting a right into law. (Inalienable rights going through the same stages would keep their truth-value, for enactment then consists of increasing the legal effect of a right already held to exist.) Do the championings of a right that is so to speak separated from truth-values on occasions falling *within* the process of formal enactment have truth-values beforehand? If the championings are in a form of words that expresses a categorical declaration of right, I think they do; for people would argue that such a right already can be gathered from existing laws or customs. So would the truth of the complex rule to which the declaration of right corresponds. Nevertheless, the right may need formal recognition by enactment; and in the course of enactment it is clearly within the powers of the people and the government together (as they themselves believe) either to confirm the right or to discard it. After enactment, declarations of right (outside the official statute books) have truth-values depending on evidence or implications of enactment. Setting forth then amounts at least to stating certain propositions; in the paradigmatic cases of rights, it amounts as well to endorsing the rights morally.

Qualifications to the Thesis of Double Variation. On the view here taken, a right is always either legal-in-fact or legal-in-intention. This thesis now needs to be qualified, but not so qualified as to give credence to the common view of legal rights and moral rights as constituting two separate corpuses. Nor should the thesis be qualified by any concession to the familiar philosophical doctrine that sometimes "N has a right to do *a*" means merely "It would not be wrong for N to do *a*." This doctrine, working hand in hand with the very frequently observed discrepancy between what are championed as rights and what are recognized as rights by law, induces people to adopt the two corpuses view.

The doctrine, however, is unfounded; the discrepancy has another explanation.

Weak Interpretation of Rights Rejected. It is never the case that "N has a right to do *a*" means merely "It would not be wrong for N to do *a*." If the latter statement is all that is meant, then uttering the former sentence is a mistake (even if it happens fairly frequently). Changing from asserting a right to saying that it is not wrong always involves stepping down, waiving the callings upon specially directed at M and other people. Changing from saying that it is not wrong to asserting a right to do *a* always involves stepping up, raising special callings upon not previously in question, though these may still have to be spelled out.

One can feel the force of the change everywhere. N has lent his car to M for the day now over. It would not be wrong for N to take the car back; but if only this could be said, it would not be wrong, either, for M to keep it. N has a *right* to take the car back. N has a right to a fair trial; having it, he would be remarkably unwise to settle for the concession that it would not be wrong for him to have a fair trial. N has a right to look at M's diary, and so may expect M's secretary to make it available; if it were merely a case of its not being wrong for him to look, given that he has a good reason to, everything would depend on the secretary's good will. It would not perhaps be wrong for N to attend classes at X, a school for Catholic children; but that is a far cry from his having a right to attend classes there.

Are there not some instances in which not being

wrong to do *a* implies having a right to do it? Does not the implication sometimes perhaps run the other way as well and at the same time, so that we can both infer "has a right" from its not being wrong, and its not being wrong from "has a right"? I doubt whether there are in fact any cases of this double-connection. Having a right amounts to having in hand a special social device; but however the use of this device is circumscribed, it cannot be guaranteed never to be used in ways that are morally objectionable. Human knowledge and foresight, as embodied in the construction of social devices, do not extend so far. N may have a right to marry a certain girl—he is not tied; she is not; they are both healthy; both are of age; she has freely given her consent—yet it may transpire that it is wrong for him to exercise his right in this case. Perhaps the discrepancy in their ages is objectionable; perhaps marriage will prevent either or both of them from pursuing careers of greater benefit to mankind.

Even if instances could be found in which the double-connection held, its not being wrong and having a right would be perfectly distinct in meaning in those very instances. For what would the double-connection amount to? It would amount to the truth-conditions for "It would not be wrong for N to do *a*" happening to coincide in those instances with the truth-conditions for "N has a right to do *a*." Thus, on the one hand, we would on those conditions be prepared to say, in effect, "N is not to be morally condemned for doing *a*" (which is roughly what "would not be wrong" means); on the other hand, on the same conditions, here functioning as the third part of the rules corresponding to a right, we would assert, in effect, the existence of the exercise and status aspects, the first and second parts of the rules, and with them the requirements for cooperation and noninterference. The conditions are the same; but the two pronouncements that we would make are utterly different.

Probably there are several ways of distinguishing even highly generalized assertions of rights from mere denials of wrongdoing. One interesting way follows from distinguishing in matters of skill and in competitive situations between attempting and achieving: "It is not wrong to do *a*" applies equally well to attempts and to achievements: it is equally not wrong to cry up one's goods and to sell the whole lot of them; to study German and to master it; to work on brake design and to invent an improved braking system; to enter a race and to win it. In such cases, however, one can have rights only to attempting, not to achieving. (Sometimes the crucial verbs are ambiguous between attempting and achieving: the streethawker has a right to sell his toys—if he can.) The reason is not far to seek: to require the actions of other people that would defend and guarantee N's achieving such things would either be absurd, as beyond human capacity, or would destroy the species of interaction in question: bring the game to an end, or close off opportunities for economic competition.

Two Corpuses Theory Rejected. As for the frequent discrepancy between rights morally endorsed and rights legally recognized, this has two sides: the cases where people affirm certain rights as matters of law, without meaning to endorse them morally; and the cases where people endorse certain rights morally, without meaning to imply that they are already matters of law. There is, of course, no discrepancy in the central cases where the rights are both matters of law and morally endorsed.

Is it to be supposed that in such central cases there are two sets of rights, moral rights and legal rights, which here fortunately happen to match? The two corpuses view is not an economical explanation. Moreover, it leaves one to grope in separate spheres for moral rights as against legal rights, without furnishing any instructions about where the sphere of moral rights might be looked for. Turning away from the two corpuses view to the view adopted above, one beholds rights ascending from championship to full recognition, moral and legal simultaneously; and then, in some cases, with the passing of time, losing their moral force while they retain a foothold in the letter of the law. This conception dispenses with dispensable mysteries and stimulates inquiries correctly aimed at historical processes of debate, innovation, and decay.

The thesis that a right is always legal-in-fact or legal-in-intention nevertheless requires qualification in at least two connections. In the first place, the law in question may not be the law of government and the courts of justice, but the law of other institutions— of the church, for example; or of a university, relating either to its faculty or to its students. The law in some of these institutions has provisions for testimony and adjudication as elaborate and continuous as in the courts of justice. The parallels of course vary from firm to faint. A grievance procedure, voluntarily conceded by management to nonunion employees, will be less lawlike than canon law, enforced by ecclesiastical courts; though grievance procedures established in a union contract would not suffer from the comparison. The rules of a private club may be very informal; the customs of a family would in most families hardly be codified at all. Yet even in a family there may be something enough like the conception of a legal system for parents and children to have mutually acknowledged rights, adopted within their own house-hold.

In the second place, there are some cases of rights that are championed, even acknowledged as fully as they are ever going to be, without there being any intention of making them matters of law, whatever kind of law or institution might be in question. Such, for example, is the right of a friend about whom you have expressed suspicions to obtain a hearing from you. More certainly is at issue here than its not being wrong for him to have a hearing; it would be absurd to suggest that there was not more. Yet, almost equally clearly, people would be reluctant to make such a right a matter of law, itself to be enforced by pro-cedures for formal hearings, compulsory process for witnesses, adjudication under pain of a judge's dis-pleasure. Litigation would kill the friendship, which your suspicions have only jeopardized.

Both these qualifications, sized up overquickly, tend to give new life to the two corpuses view. Are not rights that are never meant to be law members of one corpus only? Are not rights connected with systems of rules not fully legal best thought of in the same way? The two corpuses view, however, simplifies matters in a complex field of topics without anything like due regard for the structure of the field. In that structure rights simultaneously morally endorsed and legally affirmed are central. All other rights are to be understood as approximations of these. When I say, "Your friend has a right to have a hearing from you," I mean that you, though not in fact under legal com-pulsion, should accord him the right as if it had the force of law.

Not All Rules of Interaction Rules for Rights. The rules corresponding to rights differ, then, from other rules of interaction not only in their relation to systematic compulsion; but also (a connected matter) in their relation to law. The latter relation is consciously and intentionally one subject to a double variation, of moral and legal force, attaching to the callings upon set forth in the rules. One might well ask, might not this double variation be accepted as applying to all callings upon and all rules of interaction? The answer seems to be that it might be; with some precautions taken against incompatible prescriptions, all rules of interaction might be intended as matters of law, even of governmental law, with legal compulsion attaching to them. All of the examples of callings upon mentioned above as not having the force of rights could be recast by innovation so as to have that force. One might imagine a society taking pitch-and-catch so seriously that the man who stepped aside instead of trying to catch the ball would be taken to court in disgrace. There are societies where what might seem to us mere matters of courtesy would be treated as sacred rights: there the spurned hand would turn to litigation, or to the sword. The hawker might be given the right not merely to sell his toys—if he can—but to force sales of them on each of his auditors.

Innovation has not in fact gone to such lengths. There are plenty of social rules that in fact fall outside the concept of rights. It is lucky that there are, because it would turn out to be extremely inconvenient, if innovation were carried to the limits of what might be sanctioned as rights. The resulting system of inter-action would be rigid beyond anything yet dreamed of in human societies. No discretion would any longer be left to the expected or hoped-for respondents: their reciprocal roles would be ordained by law, without any room for mercy or charity or even kindness. (Would we ever say except mockingly that it was

"kind" of a man to respect the rights of others?)
Where it was not desired to have the reciprocation
exacted from M as a matter of right—as it would not
be in the case of the streethawker; as it would not be,
one supposes, in the case of every possible suitor for
any given lady's favors—the possibility of N's initiating
interaction would have to be cut off. The result would
drastically impoverish social life on the side of interpersonal initiatives, and stifle any chance of freedom
or discretion on the side of interpersonal responses.

1.4. Rights as Rule-Utilitarian Devices

The person holding the right is the person (normally) entrusted with deciding whether or not it shall
be exercised. If it is an alienable right, and he has not
forfeited the status associated with it by some crime,
he is the person to decide whether or not it shall be
alienated. Rights function like moral or legal instruments, distributed to the people (normally) most concerned with invoking them, whether to protect themselves in the exercise of the rights or in the associated
status.

The valid assertion of a right is (normally) conclusive against speculation about the possible consequences of heeding or not heeding the right asserted.
It is also normally conclusive against general consideration of such consequences even when the considerations are *not* speculative. An agent, faced with
an assertion of right bearing upon him, cannot excuse
himself by saying that the general happiness might
possibly be advanced by disregarding the right. He
cannot even excuse himself by saying truthfully that
several unfortunate things are likely to happen if the
right is not disregarded, so unfortunate that the con-

sequences of disregarding it will probably be better than the consequences of respecting it.

Like other remarks that I have been making, this remark rejecting excuses needs to be qualified with the word "normally." If the consequences of disregarding a right would be a final and irremediable disaster, obviously not anticipated when the right was recognized previously, the agent would be excused for disregarding it in that particular case.

However, one of the basic principles behind the practice of asserting and heeding rights is precisely to forestall general considerations of happiness or well-being and the like from being freely invoked to decide the particular cases embraced by rights. Neither the person asserting the right nor the agent or agents called upon to respect it would normally be able in a particular case to review the alternative possibilities and their consequences really thoroughly. It would be dangerous to empower agents to act on such reviews as they can make: dangerous not only because the agents are liable to bias in their own interests, deviating from the demands of the asserted right in making the reviews; but dangerous also because the agents involved are out of communication with one another and do not have the information necessary to coordinate their actions. Hence some gains obtained by individual agents' disregarding a certain right, taking these violations one by one, may be canceled out by the aggregate losses sustained by the persons holding the right (and by other people).

As devices for protecting personal interests rights are imperfect, because as it turns out, they conflict with one another in unanticipated instances; and because, perhaps without such a conflict occurring, they sometimes turn out to do less than they were expected to do to protect interests, and possibly turn out in fact to do more harm than good. This eventuality may be discovered either simply by the operation of events or by reconsidering the supposedly beneficial features of the devices. What seemed to be net benefits may not be found to be so when a correct view is taken of the relevant utilitarian considerations. (Rights are thus rule-utilitarian devices, subject in the appropriate circumstances to adoption upon act-utilitarian review.)

One might imagine such imperfections—conflicts of rights with rights, conflicts of rights with welfare— being dealt with by periodic general legislative sessions embracing or representing the whole community to which the individual persons, holding rights and heeding rights, belong. They are forestalled from acting independently to correct the imperfections; but they may act together and legislate in response to them. General utilitarian consideration of consequences, if it were ruled out in individual cases, would then only be postponed until the next legislative session. In that session the rights in question would be modified for future use, and perhaps some sort of compensation would be arranged for those who had unexpectedly suffered from the exercise of the unmodified rights in the past.

This imaginary picture is of course much too tidy. Legislation does visibly occur and visibly affect the scope and existence of particular rights. Overshadowing the formalities of legislation, however, are larger-scale historical processes of debate, fashion, obsolescence, piecemeal reorganization. Much about these processes is obscure. Such debate as men carry on about rights is intermittent. Favor or disfavor for given rights may depend not so much on debate anyway as on motivations unacknowledged or unperceived.

Whatever their nature, historical processes gradually raise up new rights to fixed positions and simultaneously undermine the rigid position of old ones (though not necessarily of all old ones). Meanwhile, however, the chief way out of rigidity lies in the discretion accorded to the holder of a right as to exercising it or forbearing to exercise it. In addition to explicating rights by exhibiting the corresponding rules, one needs to give bi-normative instructions for the use of the concept of rights—bi-normative, because they are normative at a second stage, applying to actions (speech-acts) themselves normative. Besides pointing out that the concept of rights was decentralized in administration, thus imposing on every right-holder normal responsibilities for initiative, these instructions would stress that it is not always good to exercise one's rights. Frequently, doing so exemplifies priggish, selfish, even callous conduct.

Inalienable Rights Again. The justification of particular rights requires empirical evidence about effects promoting human interests in ways conducive to general welfare. This evidence is fallible; it therefore demands periodic review. How, then, can there be inalienable or inextinguishable rights? Logically, what may have been a justified right a generation ago may no longer be justified. Would it not be perverse to safeguard any right from all attempts at relegislation? Perverse, one would think, and very likely futile; for the long-term, large-scale historical processes that raise up certain rights and wear away others will go on notwithstanding and may affect any right that one cares to name.

A right is inalienable or inextinguishable because people understand it to be so. Reflecting carefully on such a right, they would reject a rule containing provisions for alienation or extinction as not offering a correct analysis. But why should people, choosing to understand certain rights in this fashion, put the rights out of reach to themselves or to other people, as regards giving them up or abolishing them? Historically, no doubt, the chief reason has been the conviction, already mentioned, that the rights in question originate with God or in nature. Even without this conviction operating, however, men may regard certain rights as inalienable, considering that the rights in question have emerged from profound social processes worth continuing respect. If the rights themselves are morally enlightened, this respect may not be misplaced; the rights may be touchstones for moral enlightenment. The fact that they are inalienable rights does not perhaps entail that they are enlightened; but the fact that they are enlightened may reconcile people to their being inalienable.

There is, furthermore, an impressive empirical consideration that offers a strong defense, indefinitely continuing, for the inalienability of certain rights. Mindful of the weaknesses of human nature, and aware of the imperfections of provisions for legislation, people believe they will be safer if certain rights are kept out of reach. They choose to regard some rights as inalienable, perhaps because they know that on almost any issue people can be frightened or deceived into giving oppressors a show of consent. They choose to regard some rights as inextinguishable, because they do not entirely trust the motives or discretion of people in power, or their own capacity to control legislation. They may be very uncertain about some of these matters; but this uncertainty might itself be a reason for taking precautions.

Some rights, it might be said, are inalienable and inextinguishable for reasons that no empirical evidence could upset. Could the alienation or extinction of the right to a fair trial be accepted under any social conditions? It is at least misleading to answer "Yes" to this question. One may point out that it would be possible for a society not to have trials at all, either because it had eliminated crime and conflict or because it depended entirely on other methods for dealing with them. One can argue that societies are imaginable—hard, but not impossible for us to describe—which may have provisions for trial and other familiar features of our own society, but which do not have any concept of rights. Yet it seems to be true, nevertheless, that if a society makes any use of the concept of rights to regulate its affairs, then in that society there must be a right to a fair trial (or at least, to a fair hearing) in controversies about other rights, a right inalienable and inextinguishable. There must also be any other rights logically indispensable to the just administration of any scheme of rights whatever.

2 / Rights Particularized
as Major Tests
of Government

2.1. The Rights Chosen to Be Democratic and Transcultural

Major Tests by Leading Particularized Rights. What rights shall the advocate of democracy choose to make most prominent use of in evaluating governments? Some rights he will have no use for, because they do not consort (nowadays) with his beliefs in human freedom and dignity: such will be certain feudal rights; or the right, implied by Article IV, Section 2, Paragraph 3, of the Constitution of the United States, of a slave-owner to have an escaped slave returned to him. The advocate of democracy will still be left with a bewildering variety of rights to choose from. Generalized rights are likely to seem suspiciously vague—like the supposed right to freedom; particularized rights seem liable to instantaneous *ad hoc* proliferation. If one admits that a man has a right to do what he wants to in his spare time (assuming that what he wants to do does not injure others), must one also concede that he has a right to play water polo, and a right to imitate a seal barking, and a right to cast popcorn into the sea?

Shall the rights to be stressed be inalienable and inextinguishable ones? I think that it is a mistake to suppose so, if supposing so underrates the possibility of making effective use of other rights in evaluating governments. A right to abstain from bearing arms may not be inalienable or inextinguishable; yet whether or not a government respected the exercise of such a right by conscientious objectors would be a significant test of its moral practices. I think that it is equally a mistake to suppose that, within the class of inalienable and inextinguishable rights, chief or exclusive stress should be placed on the logically indispensable ones. The rights that represent empirical precautions may supply the means of equally important and searching tests. So may rights relatively particularized, as compared with rights more generalized: the fact that the latter may lend themselves more readily to forming systematic accounts of rights than the former does not make them more arresting politically. It cannot be denied that some light is to be gained from trying to work out systems of rights, implying systems of tests; but tests by rights can be significant and important without systems to support them.

Rights involve rules of interaction; but the content and variety of rules of interaction varies between societies, as does the choice, among rules of interaction, of those to be invested with the concept of rights. Rights are thus relative to social systems to a degree that other moral concepts (like justice, for example) are not. This fact suggests simultaneously that the advocate of democracy needs to locate rights that are as widely relevant, to as many societies as possible; and that he is going to have some difficulty in locating such rights. One society may be so different from another that the network of role and status relationships in which the rights familiar to the first function simply cannot be found in the second. To cite rights drawn from the first when the second society is in view may be no more sensible than citing the rules of parchesi at a billiards tournament.

The difficulty may seem to call for the discovery (or invention) of rights that are highly generalized not only respecting N and M, the persons holding the right and the persons who must heed it in status and exercise, but also respecting the range of actions that the right entitles N to perform. In this connection, the advocate of democracy may well be tempted, following glorious precedents, to found his evaluations upon a universal right to liberty.

It seems to me that this is neither the most effective way to use the concept of rights nor the best way to promote liberty. No practical society in which conflicts occur and scruples vary could grant a right to liberty without hedging it about with limitations. People could not even be permitted to do whatever they might be inclined to do, let alone assisted and protected in doing it. What is crucial for advocates of democracy and other people concerned with liberty, then, is what limitations a given government and society impose on it, according to what principles of limitation. A society that unanimously and enthusiastically agreed to a right to liberty, but which drastically limited the right in every direction, would not be so free and attractive a society as one that was more hesitant about accepting liberty as a right, but also more gingerly about putting limitations on it. Such a society might be restrained by a right more particularized than a universal right to liberty. Such a right might do so much for the concerns of freedom that it would become redundant to champion liberty as a right.

Would such a right be applicable, however, to a

wide variety of societies and governments? This question, like the possibility of finding such a right anywhere, might have to be treated speculatively, as many philosophers seem inclined to treat it anyway. As it happens, there is no need to treat it speculatively. There is a leading historical example of such a right— a right less than fully generalized respecting range of actions; yet in some forms of society at least a strong defense of liberty against unwarrantable limitations. It has been understood as an inalienable and inextinguishable right, though it is not logically indispensable to the administration of every scheme of rights whatever.

The right in question has proved applicable to a considerable variety of societies in the past; it is still applicable to a considerable variety. It is less cogent and far-reaching than it used to be; but given the amount of success that it has enjoyed, it deserves and invites experimental treatment as a point of departure for finding something better. By identifying the failures of application that now beset it, we can put ourselves in a position to see what modifications or substitutions are needed to carry on the work that it has done.

2.2. The Right to Private Property

What is this right? It is the right to private property, as John Locke, by far the most influential single author on the subject of political rights, has commonly been understood to have represented it. Locke's doctrine of private property has been much discussed, and various points in it have been widely and fervently adopted, even by people (like the Marxists) who have repudiated it by name. The simplified version that has prevailed in American thinking leaves out of account Locke's complacency about class divisions between propertied people and unpropertied people. The simplified version, therefore, displays something like universal attractions, but easily lends itself to hypocritical uses, for example, in its assistance to vulgar economic arguments for *laissez-faire*. How much can the right of private property do for the masses of people without any property to speak of, as compared with what it does for the few who have property enough to live on, and more? Marxists have rejected the right of private property in the means of production; and some of them have gone on to discard all notions of rights whatever as (so they say) obsolescent bourgeois devices.

I am bound to say, however, that neither the critics nor the champions of Locke's doctrine have sufficiently considered how effective the simplified version of the doctrine has been in providing an instrument for political evaluation. I do not think that it is widely appreciated (at any rate, appreciated nowadays) how well it once served the cause of freedom, or precisely how. Once these things are recalled, it will be clear how the work of the doctrine could be carried on by a right suited to present conditions; and clear also that the concept of rights may usefully survive capitalism, whatever abuses capitalism may have made of it.

The State of Nature. Locke asserts that in a state of nature, where there are possibly no persisting forms of social cooperation other than individual family households—where, indeed, even these do not for the purposes of the argument require much attention if any—there is a right to private property. This is Locke's way of ushering in his doctrine that any government whatever needs to be evaluated by comparison with the advantages of having this right in the state of nature. It is also a way of introducing the right for a further purpose that Locke had in mind, which was to compare forms of government among themselves by reference to their advantages in respect to this right over the state of nature. Locke's thinking about the right to private property begins, however, not with the state of nature, but with the right to private property that he found in use within his own political society and others like it. Locke extrapolates the historic, positive right to property, found always in association with organized society and government, to a state of nature from which by hypothesis, explicit and implicit, government has vanished (along with much else). But how can it make sense to do this, when we consider that a right embraces various social relationships and cannot be understood detached from its implications as to social role and social status?

Skeleton-Form of Right. The answer is that Locke seizes upon circumstances in which the right to property can be established with a minimum of prior or present social relationships: circumstances in which, as with fish in the sea ("that great and still remaining common of mankind"), there are common resources that anyone can have for the trouble of taking. Defined for such circumstances, the right to property would embrace a minimum of conditions referring to social relationships: no references to *prior* social relationships; very little in the way of references to present and future relationships. Now, the state of nature represents a generalization of the circumstances in which the right to property can be invoked in this stripped skeleton-form. Extrapolating the right of property to the state of nature, Locke extrapolates it in this form, treating the stripped down formula as the basic skeleton of the right as we know it, fleshed-out and clothed with the complications of civilization (which are reflected in the familiar conditions to be spelled out in the corresponding rules). With the form, he extrapolates the minimum required in social relationships.

The skeleton of the right to property consists of this: the right applying in the case of somebody wishing to keep for his own use something that he has made in his own free time with materials and tools his own to begin with or free for use and taking. Imagine a man spending part of his Sunday off searching through a public woodland for a birch shoot of just the right diameter; cutting it down—on the justified assumption that in this stretch of woods anyone is free to do this; taking it home and in spare hours over the next week or so, carefully whittling a birch flute. How outrageous it would be—what a clear instance of violating a right—for someone (say, a government official; indeed, anybody) to come along then and seize the flute!

The fact that such an action would arouse so much moral feeling should caution us against thinking that applied even to this amateur flute the skeleton of right is trivial. Moreover, the feeling in question springs up without waiting on further explanation. It is obviously, directly, intuitively *wrong* for anyone else to seize the flute, when the flute has originated in the circumstances described (so we feel).

The flute-maker establishes his right to the birch flute by performing the *labor* of making it. Within organized society, the man who has used his Sunday off and his spare time to perform this labor would thereby have established his *status* as owner of the flute. He performs, in performing the labor, certain actions which other people can witness (or infer from what they do witness), and this as the rule for the right to the property would show, suffices. The fact that it suffices shows that right-establishing roles need not, though they often do—as in the case of a parent caring for his children—involve doing something *for* the people on whom the rights later chiefly call.

No prior social relationships need be referred to in vindicating the flute-maker's right. The present social relationships, at the minimum, demand only that other people be able (in principle) to discover that the labor was performed and that the conditions about the availability of time and resources were met. The social relationships chiefly and characteristically involved are relationships *subsequent* to the flute-making: noninterference with the maker's possession and innocent enjoyment of the flute; assistance to the flute-maker in exercising his right and maintaining his status. But these relationships imply nothing about the presence of organized social forms of cooperation: the bearing of the right is simply universalized to all other persons as individuals.

The skeleton-right to private property, founded on labor, may (as we have seen) invest possessing even a plaything with moral concern. Locke redoubles the concern by associating the skeleton-right not with playthings but rather with the very means of life—food and other necessities. He represents the skeleton-right as protecting things that men cannot do without and that in the state of nature they can acquire only by labor. Now, it is with this double association that we, too, commonly think of labor and property, when we think of the one leading to the other. Men—most men, even in a capitalist society—must labor to live; and what they obtain through labor they deserve to keep for their own use, both because they have worked for it and because typically they need it.

The connection of the right to property with the performance of labor thus evokes a number of profoundly moving moral considerations, not stopping with the immediate outrage that violating the skeleton-right does to our intuitions. We feel, as Locke's contemporaries felt, that a man deserves to have what he has worked to have—so long as in working, he has not interfered with other people in *their* labors. This feeling is quite as prevalent among communist thinkers and in communist societies as in liberal democracies; indeed, its prominence in Marx's theory of exploitation can be regarded as an inheritance from Locke.

We also tend to feel that a person does not deserve to have what he has not worked for, supposing that he is capable of working. This feeling, too, is reflected in the thinking of Marx and his followers: during the building of communist society workers' earnings will be proportional to the amount (and quality) of their labor; once a communist society has been built, there will be no problem about deserts, because then there will be abundance and furthermore no problem about motivation or energy.

Right to Acquisition Through Labor. Behind the right that labor establishes to a specific item of property there stands another right that it presupposes—namely, the right to perform the labor that will establish property in various specific items. If the right to do the work is not respected, then (except under specially unrealistic assumptions about the goods once acquired being plentiful, durable, and inheritable) the right to keep or use the products of work (certainly, of one's own work) will soon become an empty form.

We may say, in accordance with Locke's argument (though he does not make the present distinction), that these rights, taken together, justify a man in defending the means of subsistence that he has gathered or cultivated. Considerations of defense would in turn justify the use of sufficient force against any offender to deter him from repeating a violation. "The right to private property" may be taken as referring to the combination of these rights; or to anyone's right to any specific item in which he has property, so long as it is understood that this right presupposes the right of acquisition through labor.

Whereas the right of property in a specific item is as alienable as anything could be, the right of acquisition through labor is I think an inalienable right. Yet it may be inoperative. The conditions under which it can be exercised may not be fulfilled: there may be no resources free for the taking, no spare time, no tools for anyone to use. Moreover, whether or not these conditions are fulfilled, the right to acquire property through labor may not in some circumstances have the central importance that it does in Locke's conception of the state of nature (and of the range of governments which are to be tested by considering this right and its companion right, the right to property in the specific items acquired). Subsistence—indeed, the means of a very comfortable standard of living, including the means of amusement—might be provided for socially without this right being recognized or referred to: e.g., people are invited to work for the pleasure of it; a sufficient proportion do so to keep the economy going; the output is distributed according to need.

Locke describes the economy of the state of nature variously as a food-gathering one or a farming one, in which settled cultivation is practiced. It might equally well be, in whole or in part, a hunting or a pastoral economy. (Locke treats the pastoral economy of Abraham and Lot as having important features of the state of nature.) What is essential is that it be an economy of wholly self-supporting people (or, better, self-supporting households) who do depend on the right of private property being respected; but who given this respect would have *no need for government*, and in fact no need for organized cooperation (beyond the household level) in any form.

One might ask about improvements in technique. Must there not be social organization to communicate and accumulate improvements? However, these self-supporting people need not lack means of communication; improvements might spread by example and imitation. Would not people sometimes need the help of others, when they were struck by some calamity? For example, a farm family loses its house to fire during the winter. Yet this family and others might choose to take their chances of surviving calamity by their own efforts. Human powers are such that they have something like a reasonable chance of doing so, if their efforts are not interfered with, even in the absence of anything like an organized system of reciprocal helpfulness in which they and their neighbors participate. Spontaneous charity on their neighbors' part need not be ruled out; but it need not be depended on either.

Advantages of Government Relative. If people in the state of nature might get along without government, why does government start up? Locke's aim in considering the state of nature is to reach a position from which he can invoke a basic principle for evaluating governments in terms of their use and function. The principle is this: For a government to be acceptable, people must be better off for having it than they would be not having any government at all. "No rational creature can be supposed to change his condition with an intention to be worse" (§ 131). To give people grounds to change from the state of nature to social life under government, the government adopted must offer net advantages that the state of nature does not have.

Possibly none of the governments proposed would offer net advantages. On this point Locke (at least, simplified Locke) evidently clashes with Hobbes, who inclines to hold that men are better off under any form of government whatever than without any government at all. But to make out his side of the issue, Locke need not indulge himself in hyperbole about the advantages of the state of nature; he need not be naively optimistic about human friendliness and forbearance; he need not even minimize the disadvantages of the state of nature. It suffices for him to hold that while some governments do not offer a balance of advantages greater than those obtainable in the state of nature, others do.

Governments (some forms of government) are useful because in fact the right to property is not universally and uniformly respected in the state of nature. At this point the issue posed by contrasting Hobbes' views with Locke's can be restated as involving a disagreement about the *extent* to which there will be trouble about respecting the right to private property in the state of nature. Locke grants that in fact there will be considerable trouble. So the institution of a suitable form of government will be useful: it will bring the advantages of definitely formulated laws; impartial judges to apply them; combined force to enforce them. A Hobbesian might say that there will be so much trouble without government that *any* form of government would be beneficial. Simplified Locke would have to disagree; but in doing so, again, he is not being naively optimistic about human nature. At worst, he is taking one side of an indeterminate issue;

and in fact he can reason quite plausibly on the side that he takes.

Whether a particular government is acceptable or not depends then, in Locke's view, on how well it passes the test of maintaining and protecting the right to private property. This right the citizens would have anyway, without government. Government offers them no advantages over the state of nature if it does not make the defense of this right more assured.

One might wonder whether governments do not offer numerous other advantages: institutional support for enterprises of all kinds—e.g., irrigation; institutional "insurance" against various calamities; schools, highways, national parks. But one must not foist upon Locke our modern tendency to think of any social enterprise carried on by the same institutions that exercise police powers as features of "government"; one must also remember Locke's near silence on the general subject of organized forms of social cooperation. For Locke, a government properly has the strictly limited function of protecting the property of the citizens—in which Locke includes (however awkwardly) their lives and liberty. Government, in Locke's conception, is (where it is an acceptable government) nothing more nor less than a property owners' mutual protective association and its job (apart from defense against external enemies) is confined to police work.

Locke's Doctrine Applied to America. This conception of government—already deeply entrenched before *laissez-faire* theories about limited governments in industrial economies appeared to reinforce it—has had, and continues to have, a remarkably strong grip on the part of the world to which in Locke's time—and for some time after—Locke's doctrine of property best applied. This was America, so long as America continued to be a country in which self-supporting, subsistence farmers could be reckoned as typical citizens; and so long as a surplus of natural resources remained free for the taking on the frontier. (Free, perhaps, only if one ignores the Indians; but Locke was inclined to regard the Indians as being in the state of nature, where the pioneers joined them.)

Long before they heard of *laissez-faire* economics, Americans were convinced that government ought to be limited government—limited to police functions (the companion function of external defense was conceded, but was for a long time relatively unimportant) and frugal in carrying them out. Any enlargement of government, so conceived, meant an increase in police power, hence a threat of tyranny. Police power remaining the same, an enlarged budget inevitably suggested corruption, on the part of the very people who (as monopolizing the common force of the society) had the most profitable opportunities for corruption and who were simultaneously the people whom it was most important to keep from being corrupted.

Defects and Achievements of Locke's Doctrine. Whatever its limitations, the simplified version of Locke on property is a remarkably coherent and persuasive doctrine; it is no wonder that it has been so much cherished. Even its defects assist its persuasiveness. By omitting to consider the advantages of other social enterprises besides police work (and external defense), the doctrine enormously simplifies the test that governments are to be put to, and hence the task of evaluation. For, possibly the inception or at least the success of those other social enterprises would depend on the initiative and encouragement of institutions that enlarge upon government narrowly conceived and yet are usefully managed by the same organs.

Then the advantages of political society vis-à-vis the state of nature would have to be determined by a complex balancing of different sorts of advantages; and some inefficiency in police work (indeed, conceivably, some infringements of the right to private property) might be offset by benefits flowing from other, associated functions. Locke's approach bypasses these formidable complications.

Another defect that might be found in Locke's doctrine, with its narrow conception of government and radically simplified test by the right to private property, is the encouragement that it offers to extreme individualism. Pressed to the extreme (farther than Locke himself pressed it), the doctrine implies that an individual member of the property owners' mutual protective association would owe nothing to the association that would not immediately be canceled by the failure of the association to protect his right of private property. (It is true that even so it would be unreasonable to count a momentary and remediable lapse as a definitive and irrevocable failure; but this can be assumed allowed for.) Any attempt on the part of the association to actually encroach upon that right would constitute an outrageous perversion of the purposes for which he had (in effect) joined other property owners in undertaking to have a government in the first place.

Clearly, this view of government concedes very little to the claims of patriotism—to the sort of loyalty that people ordinarily feel, and are encouraged to feel, for the national groups to which they belong. The view has, in fact, very little use for group attachments of any kind. There are such things as group rights, in the rules corresponding to which N would stand for groups of people somehow connected: for example, the burgesses of Northampton, who jointly have the right to be represented in Parliament. It might be argued that governments should be as much required to respect and maintain group rights as personal ones, a diversity of groups being essential to diversity in social training and hence to diversity in personal lives. Locke's doctrine of private property, however, gives no attention to group rights, much less any weight.

One must balance the achievements of Locke's doctrine against its defects. Two of these achievements are especially instructive. Both of them depend upon the state of nature being a relevant alternative to government. Assuming circumstances where comparison with the state of nature is apposite, Locke shows how to obtain concrete safeguards for freedom without launching upon abstract perplexities about a universal and generalized right to liberty. He also shows how sensible and far-reaching a case can be made for an unqualified stress upon the instrumental nature of government. Government is not only merely an instrument; it is an optional instrument for achieving limited human purposes.

Locke's doctrine does not attempt to deal with abstract individuals, considered before conditioning begins, and demanding (as it may seem) freedom even from conditioning—that is to say, among other things, from being brought up, socialized, enculturated. The people who choose between government and the state of nature are adults who have been conditioned to take care of themselves (if they need to) by direct individual use of the resources of nature. They could emigrate to the frontier and enter the state of nature there. They are, in other words, independent persons—independent in a perfectly concrete and exemplifiable sense. It is only for such persons—people capable of being pioneers—that the question of liberty is raised; the route by which they have arrived at their characters is irrelevant. But again, the question of liberty is not raised abstractly: what is at issue is concretely whether men shall be free to support themselves under the protection of the right to private property.

The harm that can be done to them, invading this freedom, whether by other men in the state of nature or by men dressed in the authority of government, is perfectly clear. It is the harm of interfering with the self-supporting activities of individual persons. This harm is easily avoided, since there is an abundance of natural resources to which everyone willing to support himself by his own work can turn, without encroaching upon the livelihood of other people.

The idea of freedom and of a right to liberty become definite and unproblematical here just because they are largely superfluous. The chief things that one would wish to demand under the heading of liberty have already been taken care of by recognizing the right to private property. It is true that people so protected might choose not to make full use of the protection. They might be meticulously "other-directed" conformists in their lives and outlook. Nevertheless, if the right to private property is fully respected, and *only* attempts against other people's persons or property are considered crimes, every household is free to choose its own style of life.

The instrumental view of government has a familiar footing in the slogan, "Man does not exist for the state, the state exists for man." Abstractly considered, this slogan runs into the difficulty that even in societies where it is familiar people are continually being pressed to expend themselves in government service. "Ask not what your country can do for you; ask what you can do for your country." There is, in fact, a strong case to be made for the position that individual citizens, whose personal development has been fostered within the state (but here a multiservice state), receive a continuous stream of miscellaneous benefits from government and owe it some duties in return—not necessarily duties of self-sacrifice, but perhaps at least duties in which self-sacrifice is risked. The main trouble with the position is that it tends to overshadow the instrumental aspects of government. Under cover of the shadow all sorts of attempts may be made to exact undue sacrifices.

Locke's doctrine, by contrast, achieves the very great virtue of emphasizing the propriety of viewing government as an instrument of the persons who keep it up. The emphasis, it must be noted again, gives no weight to patriotism or love of country. These are no doubt real political values, but they have been so much abused that leaving them out of account may be a necessary step in removing the mystifications that politicians have practiced with them. Dr. Johnson's dictum that patriotism is the last refuge of a scoundrel has been extensively illustrated in our own day by noisy figures in the United States Congress. Locke's drastically unsentimental approach at least redresses the balance with sentiment. The self-supporting farmers that Locke has in mind could make shift without their government—their mutual protective association. They set it up and keep it up entirely on a voluntary basis. If it does not serve the very limited purposes for which it is set up, the members may act together to dissolve it.

2.3. The Right to a Livelihood

Present Inadequacy of Locke's Doctrine. The things that Locke achieved by use of the right to private property may inspire similar achievements in our own day. Would the right to private property still be as useful in evaluating governments? The answer is that it would not; to achieve Locke's results in our own day, some other particular right or rights must be used. The simplified version of Locke's doctrine fit America in his day and for a considerable time there-after—through the age of the American Revolution and the time of Constitution-making. It does not fit America today.

No one could plausibly hold, of course, that the right to private property has become obsolete *per se*. Both the skeleton-right—under which N establishes his status as rightful possessor by doing work in his own time upon resources free for the taking—and the highly elaborated right familiar in capitalist so-ciety—under which N may become rightful possessor in multifarious ways involving little or no effort on his part, as by inheritance or by windfalls in the stock market—survive in tough fighting trim. (One must bear in mind that Locke's argument about the skeleton-right does not extend to justifying the elaborated right; Locke passes over the gap with scandalous negligence.)

The right to private property has remained in force. The rule corresponding to it has been elaborated fur-ther to take into account newly important forms of property—shares of corporation stock, for example. But the rule has nevertheless ceased to be a sufficient, or nearly sufficient, concrete means of defending per-sonal liberty. Nowadays, in America as in Britain, the typical member of society is very far from being a self-supporting farmer. It was not unreasonable for Americans of the generations of 1776 and 1789 to think of the typical citizen as such, either actually or with some hope of being so; but he is not today, and he has no prospect of becoming one. The typical mem-ber of modern society, in America and elsewhere, is an employee who depends for his livelihood on the continuing receipt, week by week or month by month, of a pay check. He may own property, but only relatively rarely does this consist of property in the means of production, and only more rarely still does his property amount to enough for him to live on.

Not only is the typical member of modern society an employee; he is typically an employee of some large bureaucratic organization, which is run, not on democratic principles, but by a self-perpetuating élite of top managers. In many cases these managers have only grudgingly conceded subordinate employees the right to join in collective bargaining about terms of employment. Employees whose services have been sought by other organizations have, of course, been able to use this fact as a personal bargaining advantage. Many who have the advantage in times of prosperity and full employment lose it, however—and with it their chief recourse against arbitrary action by management—when times change and jobs are hard to find. Some never have it.

One can imagine societies in which the advantage hardly exists for anyone. When the state is the sole employer, the employee may be unable to move from job to job without permission; he may have no choice of terms, because he has no choice of jobs. He might try to emigrate, but he is liable to find the frontiers closed. By comparison, a capitalist society with many employers competing with one another for employees as well as in other respects has considerable attractions. (Moreover, in a capitalist society, some people may turn out to have enough property to live on, so that they can escape intimidation from employers; and some of these people may have the courage to act freely, sometimes on behalf of the oppressed.)

Actually, even in countries with thorough-going socialist programs some freedom exists with respect to choice of occupation and within occupations with respect to choice of jobs. Different industries and enterprises, even though they are all working under the same central plan, may compete with one another for labor and strive to make the terms that they offer attractive. In capitalist countries, on the other hand, employers sometimes practice blacklisting. No doubt some of them do so without ceasing to vociferate about capitalism being the sole basis of personal freedom.

Liberty runs special dangers in a society of employees, even under capitalism, and even without blacklisting. A government that respected and maintained the right to private property would not do so much for personal liberty in a society of employees as it would do in a society of self-supporting farmers, such as Locke (simplified Locke) envisaged—and not only Locke, but the signers of the Declaration of Independence, too, and the successful proponents of the first ten amendments to the United States Constitution.

Those amendments (the Bill of Rights) restrain the United States government from, among other things, abridging freedom of speech by law and the use of the courts or by other practices capable of interfering with a person's bodily liberty or his property (like quartering soldiers in private houses or visiting private households with unreasonable searches and seizures). Protected from government action in these ways, a self-supporting farmer might make himself unpopular by expressing unexpected opinions. But must not people sometimes expect to risk unpopularity as the cost of exercising liberty? Unpopularity notwithstanding, the farmer could go on supporting himself. (The government must not only refrain from interfering with his person and property; it must go on protecting him as much as it does other property owners.)

An employee enjoys under the Bill of Rights the same protections against government action as the self-supporting farmer does; but they do not give him the same security. He must, in the first place, please his employer; and employers vary greatly in the amount of liberty that they are willing to grant their employees, on or off the job. In the second place, an employee must be careful, even if he satisfies his employer in other ways, not to become conspicuously unpopular with other people. He will lose his job and livelihood if he displeases his employer, and one way of displeasing him is to offend against "good public relations." The House Un-American Activities Committee has steadily played upon this consideration to bypass the Bill of Rights. Its subcommittees sweep through the country, calling people into the limelight of unfavorable publicity, and leaving employers to deal with these people afterward. The employers (sometimes universities that on other occasions have made resounding declarations in favor of academic freedom) have often been very willing to oblige. The result has been a trail of dismissed employees; and, one conjectures, for every dismissed employee, thousands of people who have been shut up by intimidation.

Is it much consolation to these people that this intimidation may have been practiced without ever violating the right to private property? Liberty no longer derives the effective protection that it used to have from the right to private property; and no other right has risen to serve it in the same way.

The Right to a Livelihood, a Revision of Locke. Can such a right be found? If it were found, would it have a reasonable chance of becoming fully established, as a right not merely legal-in-intention, but legal-in-fact as well, supported as nearly universally and as strongly as any right could be expected to be? I think such a right can be found. It would do approximately the work that the right to private property does in the kinds of society which Locke's doctrine envisages. It would also do this work in other kinds of society, which his doctrine does not suit. It would, of course, leave some things to be safeguarded by other particular rights, or advanced by evaluative considerations outside the concept of rights; but the right to private property in Locke's doctrine is less than comprehensive in the same ways.

A right of the kind now sought may be found by modernizing Locke's doctrine. In finding it, the significance of the concept of rights as the source of a major test of contemporary governments will be made good, and its relevance vindicated. The nature of the concept, as something susceptible of just this sort of development and reconstruction, will be further explicated. I recommend the construction, but enter upon the recommendation only as a way of pursuing the task of explication to the end—to the point, that is, of producing a definite contemporary test. Following Locke's example, we wish to obtain a concrete and particularized right, relatively easy to comprehend, relatively easy to administer in a decentralized way. The right should be effective against interferences, both on the part of government and on the part of private persons, with the most vital aspects of men's freedom—for example, freedom of speech, of association, of movement from town to town, and from job to job. Using his example as a point of departure, we wish to preserve whatever is still relevant and useful in Locke's doctrine, yet modify it (as we must modify it) for use in testing a different range of governments. In our day, the most urgent range to consider would seem to be governments in various highly industrialized societies in which the population consists predominantly of employees of large bureaucratic organizations. Both societies in which these organizations are wholly public and societies in which some of them, perhaps most of them, are private, and many or most of these profit-making, need to be covered if we are to compare, say, the governments of the United States and Canada with the most relevant alternatives.

The clue to the necessary modifications has become manifest in the reason for the success of the doctrine in the past. The reason why the right to private property succeeded in defending liberty in the past, so far as it did succeed, was that in the past respecting this right accorded typical citizens protection in their livelihood. Shall not typical citizens be accorded this protection today? Liberty and democracy might be well served by recognizing a right to a livelihood.

Just by being a member of the society falling within the embrace of a certain government, N would be entitled, if he needed training, to training that would qualify him for employment. By being a member of the society and having qualifications for employment, he would have a status, either as a jobholder or as a jobseeker, calling upon other members of the society M, in both private and public positions, to do or refrain from doing various relevant actions, like publishing information about job vacancies, and suppressing arbitrary disqualifications.

As a jobseeker, N would in exercising his right to a livelihood be calling upon various people M to try him out for suitable vacancies; perhaps he would be calling on various responsible officials M to assist him with economic policies that create jobs. If he already had a job, N's right to a livelihood would be exercised by continuing to perform the job and resisting attempts to dislodge him from it. For those exceptional people with enough property to live on, and for people with adequate pensions, the right would extend at least to protecting these sources of their income and livelihood.

I am deliberately using "livelihood" to range over ways of obtaining the means of maintaining life (perhaps, life in a decent style) rather than to refer to the means of maintenance themselves: food, shelter, clothing, etc. Hence by "a right to a livelihood" I mean "a right to a way of obtaining the means of life." I am not sure that I am thereby extending the ordinary use of "livelihood." Dictionaries tend to equate "livelihood" with the means rather than with the way of obtaining the means, and they are at least in part justified by such expressions as "getting one's livelihood." Getting his livelihood from the sea or forest or farm or factory, a man gets either income from employment there (the means of purchase) or goods that he sells for income or sometimes goods that he consumes. Even in these connections, however, to "lose one's livelihood" would mean more than to lose some stock of goods or money; it would at the very least mean to stop receiving a flow of such things, and the flow would by implication stop because the way in which the flow had been obtained no longer worked. Hence people do not merely think of themselves as "depending for their livelihood" on their properties or their professions. Speaking with only a little liberty, they *identify* their livelihoods with these things. A doctor may speak of medicine as his livelihood; a storekeeper, of his grocery or the grocery business. (Compare, "medicine" or "the store" "is his whole life.")

It seems to me that the present use of "livelihood" is complex enough to sustain thinking of the right to a livelihood as amounting to the right to obtain one's income in the way one is now obtaining it, or in some other way for which there is an opportunity, supposing it is not criminally obtained. I want to leave it open whether the right guarantees obtaining an income when one's present way fails. Without extending so far, the right would exact compensation for interferences with one's present way, and prevent interferences with seeking a new way.

If such a right were fully established—morally endorsed not just as a matter of recommendation, but morally endorsed along with being established in law —the chief extant means for intimidating people in the exercise of freedom, including their freedom to exercise other rights, would disappear. The success of Locke's doctrine in defending liberty would thus be regained, by means continuous with Locke's own. The right to a livelihood would carry on the work of the right to private property, so far as such property is still for some people indispensable to their livelihoods; and extend similar protection to people dependent for their livelihoods upon employment.

Moreover, the right to a livelihood could be invoked to renew support for the instrumentalist view of government. The comparison with a state of nature remains relevant. Admittedly, it is now (or soon will be) basically impossible for a population as large relative to resources as that of the United States to support itself in the absence of government and intermediate forms of organized cooperation. Nevertheless, reference to such self-support being possible in the past justifies the view that government was an instrument of men's purposes then. It has not ceased to be an instrument; what has happened is that it has become (or is becoming) an indispensable instrument. But the reason that it is indispensable is still founded upon its being an instrument for helping men gain a livelihood. Government is, we may say, an instrument for maintaining everyone's right to a livelihood. A government that does not maintain this right does less well by its citizens than they could do for themselves given a state of nature and sufficient resources for them to be self-supporting therein.

One might define the right to a livelihood more or less narrowly—narrowly, perhaps, to begin with, to suit the present age; more broadly later on, if general assent to broader terms were then forthcoming. Most people in most other advanced countries might assent to the broader terms straightaway; but I am not sure that most people in the United States would. A large number of Americans, who exercise a great deal of political influence, might not as of now assent very readily even to the narrower terms. If we direct our thoughts to the present age, we cannot leave these Americans out of account, however obsolete we may think their ideas are. They, too, generally count themselves as advocates of democracy; and I shall count them as such.

Narrowly defined, the right to a livelihood would stress (in the case of people without enough property to live on) qualifications, which might themselves have to be earned, and continuing qualified performance; the right would not guarantee every jobseeker a job to find, even qualified jobseekers, or every jobholder a job to keep, even diligent jobholders. The right to private property does not guarantee that resources will be abundant; the right to a livelihood does not guarantee a favorable economic climate. Narrowly defined, the right to a livelihood implies a right to a job only if a suitable job is available.

Yet such a right would not by any means be ineffective; and it is so easily reconciled with a variety of political and economic beliefs, themselves conflicting, that it raises hopes of early establishment. Even narrowly defined, the right to a livelihood should suffice to protect any jobseeker or jobholder in expressing political opinions; in keeping company off the job with anyone he likes; in leading a private life that is none of his employer's business. If the right were respected, a job could be refused to a jobseeker only if it had already been given to somebody else, equally qualified and at least equally prompt to apply for it. If the job were vacant, it could not be refused, and if it was held, it could not be taken away, for any reason other than N's failure to be qualified or his failure to perform the job.

As an employee or prospective employee, N would have to be honest; sufficiently diligent; sufficiently skillful; ready to accept the conditions associated with the job at least for the time being. He would be free, however, to differ with his employer in tastes and opinions and associations. His tastes and opinions and associations would not be reasons for taking away his private property. Carrying forward the analogy, they would not be reasons for taking away his job, considered as an alternative source of livelihood. (They would not be reasons for taking away a pensioner's social security benefits, which the United States government has stooped to do on occasion.)

The right to a livelihood in a society of employees would not, it may be conceded, be so easy to administer as the right to private property in a society of subsistence farmers. A livelihood is not, in general, such a tangible consideration as this or that particular farm. The criteria for determining whether the right to a livelihood has been respected are liable to be extremely complex—for example, as regards the question whether a given man is qualified for a certain job, or the one best qualified. The criteria for determining whether the right to private property has been re-spected are by comparison simple and straightforward —at least in societies of subsistence farmers, with just their sorts of property to consider.

Yet some important steps have already been taken to extend to employees a right to a livelihood; and these steps have initiated various sustained efforts to master the associated complications about criteria. What constitutes good reasons for denying a person a given job has been defined in part by administrative experience with fair employment practices acts. What are to be counted as good reasons for dismissing some-one from a job already held have in part emerged during the vicissitudes of administering acts protecting workers in their attempts to unionize. Unemployment insurance exists as if called into being by the right to a livelihood (though it can be argued for on other grounds). Administering the rule against paying un-employment insurance to persons who refuse suitable employment has helped to clarify notions about when jobs and qualifications match each other.

So much has been accomplished, in fact, toward establishing a right to a livelihood that taking a narrow view of it may seem an excess of caution. Is not a broad conception of the right within reach even in the United States? One might hold, indeed, that the broad conception has already been put to work. Job-less people are not left to starve; lazy persons and criminal ones (once behind bars) are accorded a liveli-hood, even though they do not earn one and their failure to earn one is their own fault. To say that the means of sustenance are given in such cases not in response to a right, but solely out of mercy and charity, seems to be cant. Criminals still have some rights even in prison—among them the right, if they have not been sentenced to death, to be kept alive.

Are people who have merely been lazy to be treated less respectfully? What about people who have not been lazy at all, but who simply cannot find work? Some of these are handicapped physically or mentally; others are able-bodied enough, but unemployed because of economic fluctuations or because technological changes have made their skills and capacities obsolete. Is not the right of all these people to a livelihood, whether or not they are working, already recognized?

Yet the time has not yet come, many people in the United States would think, to go further than the right to a livelihood narrowly defined. These people would not agree that everyone had a right to a livelihood, whether or not he was working. Everyone (at least everyone without substantial amounts of property) must either be ready to work or be rehabilitated to make him ready. Granted, humanity requires that men being rehabilitated be kept alive while the rehabilitation is going on; but it may be made a condition of their being kept alive that measures of rehabilitation be set in motion.

What, however, is to be done about men ready to work for whom no jobs are available? Those of our contemporaries who would go no further than the right to a livelihood narrowly defined would be inclined to regard unemployment of this kind either as a species of natural calamity, the victims of which might appeal to the humanity of those more fortunate, or as the effect of failing to practice *laissez-faire* economics, in which case the lack of jobs would be an unnecessary misfortune. In neither case would a right to a livelihood need to be invoked as grounds for appropriate action; and it would foster undue expectations to concede such a right as being relevant.

This opinion does not yield very readily to argument; but in the present connection one does not need to dispute it. One would jeopardize the chances of the right to a livelihood being generally accepted in the United States today if one insisted that the right be broadly defined. The best policy seems to be to maximize agreement by accepting a narrow definition.

Meanwhile technological unemployment can be remedied as a matter of humanity and welfare; and cyclical unemployment could be approached in a variety of ways, without affecting general assent to the right to a livelihood. Agreeing on such a right, narrowly defined, with the advocates of *laissez-faire*, the opponents of *laissez-faire* economics could consistently contend that the way to make jobs available was for the government to manage the economy with appropriate fiscal policies. All parties would agree on the desirability of jobs being available; once the jobs were available, the right to a livelihood would be operative.

The right to a livelihood would derive some strength from being understood as inalienable and inextinguishable. Legislators, and their constituents, would then regard it as out of their reach to deny, but imposing on them obligations to see fulfilled. (The right to a specific job would not be inalienable, of course, any more than the right to a specific item of property; one might quit the job, or forfeit one's right to it.) Even an inalienable and inextinguishable right, however, does not free people from liability to punishment and reparations for actions outside the right. The concrete strength that the right lent to the defense of liberty would depend on how this necessary concession was exploited. If everything that those in power wished to suppress were made a crime, little liberty might be left for the right to defend.

Like the right to private property in a society of subsistence farmers, however, the right to a livelihood has the virtue of suggesting a relatively narrow definition for crimes. Among those farmers, only actions involving physical harm to life, limb, or property, or attempts to seize items of property from their rightful possessors, would be reckoned as crimes, along with attempts to interfere with the prevention or prosecution of such actions. In a society of employees, the right to a livelihood would add interferences with job-seeking or jobholding—attempting to get a man fired without cause; accepting a bribe to deny him a job.

In fact, many other actions are reckoned as crimes —failure to pay taxes, for example, or violations of the antitrust laws. Some of these actions may be held to be inimical to the right to a livelihood, as failing to pay taxes is inimical by undermining the government whose task it is to maintain the right. Other crimes—like violating the antitrust laws—are harder to connect with the right to a livelihood; whatever the reasons for holding such actions to be crimes, and they may be good reasons, one must suspect that prohibiting them requires sacrifices of liberty that the right to a livelihood does not itself require or justify.

2.4. A Consolidated Test Including Other Rights

Advocates of democracy, even if they relied mainly on the right to a livelihood when they used the concept of rights to evaluate governments, would not wish to rely on this right alone. (Nor would Locke's followers have settled for the right to property alone.) They would, as history demonstrates, probably wish to protect specific liberties—like freedom of religion, of speech, of the press, of assembly—against threats that may operate directly on people without first impinging on their livelihood. The pretext of unity in collective effort, for example—"national unity"— might be cited in making such threats. Rights to free speech, to a free press, to free assembly block this pretext and others from operating. Historical experience has also shown the value of keeping up a number of particular rights regarding legal procedures—the right of *habeas corpus,* for example, and perhaps the right to a jury trial (as a means to having a fair one).

Other subjects would quickly be accorded the protection of the concept of rights if they were thought likely to be endangered. A government that (except in time of war) separated men from their wives and children would readily be condemned as violating rights to family life, though such rights are not mentioned in the best-known constitutions. Advocates of democracy are likely to become agitated about a right to move about (and beyond) the country, if they have to deal with a government that is preventing people from moving about. What presses for mentioning as rights depends partly on what sorts of dangers, obstructions, and interferences actually exist.

For all that it would do on behalf of liberty, furthermore, the right to a livelihood falls short of protecting certain sorts of freedom that there was no occasion to exercise in a society of self-supporting subsistence farmers. It does not cover citizens' rights to the free use of government services and facilities, beyond their right to the services of protection. Nor does it embrace anything like a right to use facilities privately owned but open to the public. These topics, and others, are subjects of current agitation under the heading of "civil rights." Education, participation in farm programs, the right to use buses, theaters, and restaurants on the same terms as anyone else are not covered by the right to a livelihood. They are not covered by the right to private property either. In a society of self-supporting farmers that right was not incomplete in this direction, however, as a right to a livelihood is now. There the government did not provide services like education; there were no farm programs; there were not, in Locke's basic picture, any facilities open to the public except the courts.

Finally, it will be observed that the rights so far mentioned do not include a right to participate in government, which democrats would wish to accord very broadly, to adult citizens regardless of occupation or social class. Respect for this right occurs automatically when a government passes the third test that I shall propose for democracy, the test of collective preference; and if this test is insisted upon with sufficient vigor, mention of the right to participate (including the right to vote) becomes strictly speaking redundant. Yet the right to participate might still claim support as a useful precaution. Governments unable or unwilling to pass the test of collective preference might be held to observing the right to participate as a minimum gesture toward passing the test.

The test of rights on which advocates of democracy would settle, then, will be a consolidated one, in which other rights will join the right to a livelihood. I suggest that these other rights comprise the civil liberties mentioned in the First Amendment to the United States Constitution; the right to fair treatment in the courts (which might be held to be implied by having any right whatever enforceable at law); the right to share on fair terms in the use of public facilities and in the benefits of public programs; and the right to participate in the process of government, including the right to vote. Each of these rights deserves separate discussion; just how they are best circumscribed cannot be determined satisfactorily otherwise. Of them all, how-

ever, I shall further discuss in this book only the right
to participate; and discuss that only in effect, in the
course of examining collective preference. Civil liberties, due process, and rights to civic benefits do not
languish in neglect of treatment elsewhere; nor do I,
strongly as I believe in them, have anything especially
new to say about them. To fix their character for the
present purpose of arriving at a definite test of rights,
I shall simply say that they are to be understood as
currently upheld in decisions of the United States Supreme Court. (I realize that books—other books—
could be written, indeed, are written, to explain the
significance of these decisions.)

A government will pass the present test of rights
without question if and only if it refrains from violating the right to a livelihood and the other rights on
the consolidated list; and moreover actively enforces
these rights so far as necessary. It may very well be
impossible in practice for a government to refrain or
enforce without explicitly using the term "rights" or
some term interdefinable with it; but we shall allow
theoretically for a government's passing the test simply
by coincidence of its behavior with what explicit use
of the term "rights" would have called for. If a government fails the test in respect to even one right on one
occasion, it fails the test as a whole. This perfectionist
approach may be justified by remarking how doubtful
any excuses for failure must seem. If it was not possible for the government to observe or uphold a given
right on a certain occasion, one must suspect that the
right needs redefinition; if it was possible, the government has no excuse.

The present test may serve not only perfectionist
applications to governments considered separately, but
also as a basis for comparing governments admittedly
imperfect in their performance on rights. A govern-

ment that did very badly respecting every right embraced by the test would clearly be less acceptable than a government that did almost well enough to pass on every one. Likewise a government whose performance matched another government's in every respect except that it performed badly on a right which the other government observed well enough to pass would be comparatively unacceptable. To make more refined comparisons, which would offset failures on some rights by successes on others, possibly more important, the test would have to incorporate some system of weighting. Working out such a system and defending it would lead us into complications of argument far beyond the scope of this book. So I shall leave the test of rights pretty much as it now stands, though I shall say something more in the next part about comparing imperfect governments in respect to rights.

2.5. Tests Beyond the Test of Rights

The right to a livelihood, even in combination with other rights, falls short of bringing forward all the considerations that democrats would wish to use in evaluating governments. The test of rights does not suffice; nor could it be made to suffice without serious costs in intelligibility. Rights are devices for advancing welfare; but whether or not they succeed in doing this requires considering the further subject of welfare. Rights support personal participation in expressions of collective preference; but what these expressions amount to, and how they both rest on rights and lead to policies establishing them, are considerations transcending the concept of rights.

The concept of rights, it is true, might reach farther

into these other subjects. Not everything that needs to be said about them could well be swallowed up by the subject of rights, however. It would be inconvenient to try to do everything in political life that these subjects call for doing by establishing particular rights. Perhaps it would be impossible. Consider freedom to move about the country. To be free to move, and stay moved, a person dependent for his livelihood on employment must have jobs open to move to. As an employee, he has, furthermore, a special reason for wanting to be free to move; moving is likely to be his chief recourse against the special sorts of unpleasantness that may be visited upon him by his employer. Liberty in a society of employees depends, in fact, on every employee having an alternative tolerably agreeable job to go to; or at any rate, on there being enough jobs of suitable kinds open that every employer must fear the loss of mistreated employees and subsequent difficulty in replacing them.

The right to a livelihood does not extend to guaranteeing the existence of these alternative jobs—of what amounts to super-full-employment on the demand side of the job market and, moreover, a complex variety in the surplus jobs available. One does not readily see how it could be extended. If provision for super-full-employment is possible, it is likely to be possible only as a matter of intricate economic policy. Governments may not be able to solve the intricacies. Work toward solving them, if it goes forward at all, will be carried on under the auspices of the concept of welfare, as something a government ought to do as much toward as it can, but not as one of the things that a government must do to be an acceptable government at all.

Part Two /

HUMAN WELFARE

*B*esides invoking the concept of personal rights to evaluate governments, advocates of democracy make use of the concept of human welfare. They could perhaps dispense with the concept of rights, if they accept rights simply as means of advancing welfare; they could not dispense with the concept of welfare, even though, once again, it must be noted that the concept is not used by advocates of democracy only. Other devices might, in some imaginable circumstances, protect human interests in liberty and livelihood more efficiently than any particular devices invented under the concept of rights. There is no alternative to the concept of welfare, however. Welfare supplies the basic reason for having any government or governmental device in the first place. Advocates of democracy can thus hardly escape the necessity of arguing that the governments they would judge good will promote welfare. It is, of course, nowadays commonly taken for granted that democracy does this automatically, as somehow or other it does every good thing; but before the term "democracy" grew so popular that no one could expediently denounce whatever it suggests, intelligent people did argue that other forms of government might do more for welfare. Their arguments cannot even now be dismissed without evidence.

1 / *Welfare Distinguished from Rights*

1.1. *Logically Distinct Considerations*

The considerations raised by the concepts of rights and of welfare are distinct logically. Moreover, in practice—the practice of evaluating policies and governments—they demand separate attention, because they are not constantly associated even as empirical matters. Yet the two subjects are connected in so many ways, both in fact and in supposition, that the difference between them needs to be insisted upon.

Welfare is a very broad concept. It may be held to include moral welfare as well as material welfare (though material welfare is basic); and moral welfare has something to do with rights. A person could not be said to be looking out for the moral welfare of a child if he did not observe the child's rights; inform the child of them as need be; teach the child to respect the rights of others.

These rights, again—both the child's and other people's—might be considered devices for protecting welfare; they may even have been deliberately designed to function as such devices. But if this is true—if rights are devices for protecting people's welfare—then a government's respect for rights will be a test of its effective concern for welfare. Rights might in fact be the only devices steadily operating on behalf of welfare. They might cover between them, furthermore, all the provisions for welfare yet thought of. Property, livelihood, education, the use of public facilities, health, even companionship might all be subjects wholly regulated by particular rights. To a considerable extent, they already are. In what sense, then, are rights and welfare distinct considerations?

A beginning toward seeing them as distinct considerations may be made by recalling that nondemocrats (like King John's unruly barons) may be champions of rights; yet be interested, more or less frankly, only in their own welfare, as provided for by these rights and otherwise. The rights of some people—the barons—may not at all entail, or even aim at, the welfare of other people—the people who do not happen to be barons.

Just as clearly, the welfare of one and the same set of people is a consideration distinct from their rights. For those rights—a particular assortment of particular social devices—may not suffice at all to protect their welfare. The rights of the villeins against the barons, one imagines, did not suffice (though those rights existed). The barons' own rights may not have sufficed even for barons. They may, for example, have frustrated economic innovations from which the barons would have benefited; and without these innovations the barons may have done rather poorly.

Welfare and rights are logically such different subjects that the one may be invoked while the other (without inconsistency) is disregarded. Marxist writers concern themselves with human welfare, but avoid endorsing rights for fear of compromising themselves with bourgeois ideology. One can imagine a society maintaining comprehensive provisions for human welfare without anyone ever invoking or discussing personal rights. If the provisions fail in any particular, the questions raised would be questions about efficiency; or about the adequacy of the provisions, considered as comprehensive plans.

On the other hand, people may champion rights without being interested in welfare at all, even (it may appear) their own. If they have any reasons purporting to justify the rights they champion, these reasons may be theological ones. They may say, for example, that God has imposed a system of rights and duties on men, and done so for His own good reasons, which men may speculate about, but must respect however obscure they may be. God's will is reason enough for men. Therefore a widow has a right to have her husband's brother marry her; and the brother will be punished if he refuses.

Theological reasons, unsupported by ethical ones, may not be convincing; but then it is possible to champion rights without advancing reasons at all. To the rights on a given list of rights there correspond three-part rules prescribing patterns of interaction to N, M, and other people, under specified conditions as to exercise, status, and the achievement of status. The prescriptions involved are intelligible as they stand; they may be accepted and heeded by everyone concerned without reference to reasons justifying them. Some people may never have thought of there being any need for such reasons. Others may think that no reasons could be as directly convincing to intuition as the rights themselves—certain rights. Neither of these sorts of people might be able to make a go of social organization if the rights that they had in mind were not, when instituted, compatible with considerations of welfare. But both sorts of people might be quite incurious about the question of compatibility, and quite unmindful of the fact.

1.2. Welfare as an Argument for Rights

It is possible to do without rights when arguing for welfare; and to do without welfare when arguing for rights. Advocates of democracy, however, as I envisage them, would be loath to do without either. They would certainly be eager to enlist behind the rights that they champion all the empirical support which they could get from the consideration of welfare.

One might imagine a person allying himself with democratic causes who was incurious and unmindful of welfare. His intuition may just have happened to fix upon rights of chief concern to advocates of democracy, among them the rights associated with the expression of collective preference. I think, however, that such a person would be a very untypical democrat; an ally, but not an advocate. An advocate would at least want to say that if certain rights did obviously rest securely upon moral intuition, they could also be shown to conduce to welfare. Why give up an argument that need not be omitted—and would be so dangerous to omit? Surely it would be dangerous to give men the impression that the rights advocated by democrats did not assist, and might even hinder, provisions for welfare. A sophisticated advocate of democracy would recall that there are some rights (like the right to own slaves) which democrats would repudiate, partly at least because such rights work against welfare. Mindful of the fact that current debate about rights often turns upon considerations of welfare, such an advocate would undertake to show, wherever possible, that the rights he championed would promote welfare.

A sophisticated advocate, it is true, might want to

reserve for certain rights—the right to a fair trial; or the right to equal treatment before the law—a place outside the scope of such debate. He might not be prepared to concede, or need to concede, that evidence about welfare was required to establish these rights. Here the relation might be the other way around: no evidence about welfare would be acceptable that was not collected in accordance with these rights.

Failure to collect information about certain persons, the suppression of information once collected, or distortion of the information in the process of collecting it would offend against those persons' right to be fairly considered and equally treated; or, one might say, against their right to a fair hearing. Even their right to a fair trial in a technical legal sense might be at issue; for a trial may be regarded as a means of inquiring into the welfare of the community by putting at risk the welfare of the defendants. If the evidence developed about welfare does not conform to principles of fair procedure, and the rights associated with such procedures, it will be doubtful evidence, and its implications concerning welfare will be questionable.

Even these reserved rights, however, would be demonstrably compatible with promoting welfare. A sophisticated advocate of democracy would want to show this. He would want to harmonize rights with welfare in every direction, though he would chiefly rely on the straightforward connection with those rights (like the right to private property; or the right to a livelihood) where welfare can figure as the reason for instituting the rights.

On this view, sophisticated advocates of democracy belong to one or another species of utilitarian. Which species any given advocate belongs to depends upon two things: first, on the moral prescriptions, including prescriptions about rights, which he reserves as not needing support from evidence about welfare and not risking overthrow; second, on his conception of what constitutes conclusive evidence about welfare. Some utilitarians contend that no prescriptions at all need be reserved. Others, though still leaving ample room for considerations of welfare to operate in justifying prescriptions, would want to reserve quite a lot of prescriptions from empirical determination. Some utilitarians believe that welfare reduces to happiness and happiness to pleasure; and some of these, at least in the past, have believed that the happiness of groups of people can be measured by a felicific, that is to say, hedonistic calculus. Other utilitarians do not believe either of these things; they accept the ingredients of welfare as maybe irreducibly diverse. For them (and, I think, in ordinary language generally) welfare functions as a convoy concept, within which a number of particular considerations float on their own bottoms and can be separately observed to keep up with the rest or lag behind. Among these considerations, the ingredients of welfare, figure food; safety; clothing; shelter; medical care; education; congenial employment; companionship. One can treat happiness as another particular ingredient of welfare, to be added to the convoy; or recognize that all the other ingredients mentioned contribute to making happiness possible, though happiness itself (unlike the other considerations) is rarely a direct object of social policy.

Applied to evaluating governments, the concept of welfare may be applied as stringently as the concept of rights. The failure of a government to provide for the welfare of even one person may be taken to be an outrage, sufficient to condemn it. Some people, however, would argue that the best provision for welfare that a government could make would inevitably fall short of guaranteeing everybody's welfare, for the best provision on the part of government would be to allow everybody to provide for himself. Other people, whether or not they agreed with this contention, would consider that governments (other than those of very rich countries like the United States and Canada) cannot generally be expected to have resources and techniques sufficient to guarantee everybody's welfare. Strive as it may to provide for welfare, the performance of even a very active government might fail to satisfy a perfectionist. Considering perhaps almost all governments of the past, and most governments even today, one must expect, using the concept of welfare, to be comparing imperfect provisions, and to find at most that a government is better if its provisions are less imperfect than given alternatives.

What sort of comparisons will these be? Since the project of constructing a felicific calculus has not been realized, the comparisons cannot go farther than comparing proportions in the populations affected. The comparisons must also work within the limitation that larger proportions count as improvements only if making those people happier, for example, has not involved making other people unhappier. (This limitation reflects the stringent individualism that is present in the concept of welfare as in the concept of rights, though more latent.)

The comparative approach commonly taken to welfare and to particular aspects of welfare extends easily to various particular devices for decentralizing provisions for welfare. One might compare, for example, the proportions of two populations who have the means and opportunity to take out personal health insurance. One might likewise compare the proportions of two populations whose right to private property, or right to a livelihood, was respected and maintained by the governments concerned. If, invoking the concept of rights, one concedes that it is often of interest, in evaluating governments, to discover which of two imperfect governments is the better, one will take the comparative approach. This may happen without any need to insist that the rights in question are to be regarded as means of promoting welfare. Whether or not the rights are so regarded, the comparative approach establishes another connection between the concept of rights and the concept of welfare, a connection of resemblance. It treats both as subjects for comparative judgments and requires of both the same form of evidence. But even in this treatment, the concepts do not become by any means identical in meaning.

1.3. Separate Attention Required in Practice

Welfare and rights may be logically distinct considerations, in spite of their manifold connections in familiar sorts of argument. But are they not possibly so constantly associated in practice, at any rate when it is a question of evaluating governments, that dealing with one suffices in effect to deal with the other?

Is there anything to choose between two governments equally respectful of rights and equally efficient in maintaining them? If the lists of rights were exactly the same, or at least so coincident in effect that they led to exactly the same actions and policies on the part of the governments, the people living under the two governments might still differ in welfare. Either the list of rights might not cover all aspects of welfare; or the environments in which the governments were operating might make the rights more effective in providing for welfare in one case than in the other.

Generally speaking, the lists of rights maintained may be expected to differ (though not always crucially) from one country to another. Whether they differ or not, they do in fact always fall short of guaranteeing every ingredient of welfare. The rights established in the United States at the present day certainly do not reach so far. Being able to swim, for example, is important to welfare; but there is no established right on the part of every American to be taught swimming (though perhaps there should be). Again, few things affect welfare so intimately as courtship and marriage; but no one has a right under American law to compel a girl to listen to his suit or a right to have his suit accepted. Living in similar environments under the protection of the same list of rights, or of lists equivalent in their overall protection, two populations might still differ in welfare beyond the protected range; and the same is true, perhaps *a fortiori*, if the lists of rights are not the same or equivalent.

There are thus reasons for thinking that even under governments which respect and maintain equally effective lists of rights achievements respecting welfare may vary; and hence become an additional consideration in practice. How can the operation of these reasons be escaped? It is very difficult to believe that cases will never arise in which the evaluation of a government turns on observations about welfare. One government may allow its entire population to starve, while another government does something active and effective to prevent starvation. Will not the second government be judged better than the first, never mind that both are equally devoted to maintaining lists of rights, even identical lists? The environment is something that governments are expected to cope with. Variation between governments in the sort of foresight and activity required to establish granaries has been a matter of concern since the time of the Pharaohs. It would seem clear that in practice as well as in logic all sorts of matters relevant to welfare but in fact falling outside the concept of rights will affect the evaluation of governments—not only swimming and courtship, but buying and selling, arrangements for production, firefighting, recreation; and many other things.

Difficult it may be. There are nevertheless people, of some importance as political thinkers, who have in effect persuaded themselves that in practice welfare never does need to be considered separately from rights in evaluating governments. How do they manage to persuade themselves? There are two possible lines of argument, both of which happen to deserve some respectful attention. According to one line of argument, governments are properly defined as being concerned only with maintaining rights; if some matters of welfare are left outside, to be determined otherwise than by maintaining rights, these are not to be reckoned as matters of praise or blame in evaluating governments. The other line of argument concedes the relevance of such matters to evaluating governments; on the other hand it contends boldly that if a government does limit itself to respecting and maintaining certain rights, it accomplishes as much as it can accomplish in promoting welfare.

Scope of Government Limited to Rights. The narrow definition of government, which is an inheritance from Locke and other thinkers, has a great deal of relatively recent Western history behind it, practical as well as theoretical. Some of this history was reviewed in the discussion of Locke. Governments, at least insofar as they were honest governments, used to confine themselves very largely to tasks limited to those that could at least be rationalized as maintaining rights. They did not, as a rule, build schools or hospitals; they did not develop schemes for health insurance or rural electrification; they might leave even the building of lighthouses to private organizations.

Such governments, even when they were equally zealous to maintain the same lists of rights, might of course differ in efficiency. If one government had a more alert and scientific police force than another, it would be in a position to do a better job of maintaining the right to private property. Likewise, one government might conduct its foreign policy and provide for national defense more skillfully than another. Even on the narrow definition of government this difference would count in evaluation; the difference affects the security of rights, such as the right to private property.

The tendency of the narrow definition of government is to define the practice of evaluating governments so that within this practice rights and welfare need not be separately considered. Within the practice, separate consideration would logically disappear, though the distinction in meaning between the concepts might retain the respect due it.

The tendency cannot succeed, however; the narrow definition is incapable of making it succeed. In part, the trouble with the narrow definition is that it no longer corresponds to usage. Writers as late as Marx and Engels propounded theses about government, or the state, which require interpretation according to the narrow definition—for example, the famous thesis about the state withering away after the revolution. But nowadays "the government" is understood to embrace all sorts of social enterprises very different in purpose from police work and national defense: irrigation; insurance schemes; highways; schools; parks;

research. It is hard to accept the suggestion that the government will disappear, while something like the Rural Electrification Administration takes its place. What is "the government," but the Rural Electrification Administration and multitudinous other things?

The narrow definition, even if it were not obsolete in a confusing way, would not suffice to remove welfare considerations (other than those intended to be promoted by the established list of rights) from the field. For suppose a government has been instituted simply to exercise police (and military) powers in defense of the right to private property. Once instituted, it consists of an organization that as an empirical matter may be adaptable to other purposes as well. There may be various advantages in respect to welfare in so adapting it. Waiving the question, shall we reproach the government for failing to provide for welfare in such and such ways, we may still find ourselves dealing with the question of adaptation. Shall we use this existing organization—with its powers of taxation; centralized communications; administrative experience; devices for resolving social disputes authoritatively—to perform additional tasks conducive to welfare, like establishing granaries, or providing health insurance?

Capacity of Governments to Promote Welfare. Strong believers in limited government will be inclined to shift to their second line of argument at this point. They may contend that though various advantages may be gained by increasing the tasks of government, the advantages will be outweighed by disadvantages: abrogation of rights; encroachments on liberty; in the end, reductions in welfare. This contention requires treatment as an empirical proposition—as a hypothesis of empirical social science; and it is very difficult, perhaps impossible, to obtain the empirical evidence that would resolve the issue. The difficulty of refuting the hypothesis is, no doubt, one of its chief attractions—though it is by no means a virtue in a scientific proposition to be, for all practical purposes, irrefutable. To be fair, however, one must acknowledge that besides having this attraction, the hypothesis keeps company with an elegant theory about the processes of the market, a theory that is intellectually satisfying in itself and appealing in many respects by reason of the social system it seems to imply.

Why is it so difficult to refute the hypothesis that to extend the tasks of government beyond the tasks imposed by the narrow definition will make things worse rather than make them better? Surely one can point to cases like the Great Depression in which it seems clear that if the government had not provided relief payments (whether or not it had done anything more) many people—millions of people—would have suffered helplessly.

The force of such examples may be evaded by two stratagems. First, supporters of the hypothesis may say, the systems in which breakdowns like the Great Depression have occurred have hitherto all been systems in which the government in fact had attempted to do more than the tasks maintaining rights which are its proper function. In doing more, these governments have interfered with market processes that would have prevented such breakdowns or have remedied them automatically. Supporters of the hypothesis may say, second, that in the short run painful disasters will sometimes occur—like famine, because of unprecedented drought; but even though the government might do something to alleviate these disasters in the short run, it would be better in the long run for the government not to. In the long run, the attempt to perform such tasks will be harmful; and the attempt to perform such tasks temporarily, in the short run, will lead to this long-run harm—once the government has taken on the tasks, it will be impossible to drop them. Government personnel will wish to hold on to the new powers; enlarged expectations about government activity, actual or potential, will persist in the population.

These ancillary contentions have not been refuted by observation; nor are they ever likely to be. It would be politically inexpedient to reform any going government to the point of confining it strictly and exclusively to the maintenance (say) of the right to private property. Every going government is already doing more—so much more that outcries which could not be ignored would arise from people immediately hurt by the reduction in tasks. Governments are not, therefore, going to stop interfering with market processes. Similarly, it would be politically inexpedient for a government to refrain from offering relief in short-run disasters. How long, anyway, would the long run have to be for a fair test of the hypothesis? No limit is offered; logically, it might be a thousand years away or more. No government is going to wait through a thousand years of short-run disasters in order to test a theory about the optimum relation of government and economic activity.

On behalf of not waiting, one can argue that the approximations to narrowly defined governments that have existed have encountered serious social emergencies; and that in these emergencies—for example, the potato famine in Ireland in the 1840's—adequate short-run relief could have been offered by a government undertaking an enlarged list of tasks. (In the potato famine the British government did something; but, restrained by beliefs in *laissez-faire*, not nearly so much as it could have.) Both of these assertions—that emergencies occur, even under narrowly defined governments; and that such emergencies can be alleviated by the governments undertaking further tasks—can be proved if anything in social science can be.

Can it be proved that governments which have undertaken further tasks have done more good than harm? One might expect to make some headway with this issue by considering carefully, one after another, the disadvantages to welfare that such undertakings are alleged to have created. Some may not in the end appear to be real disadvantages; others may appear, even when they are added to one another, less substantial than the advantages that offset them. Increased income taxes may have forced rich people to operate smaller yachts; but, given the increase in taxes, the government may have been able to undertake medical programs leading to dramatic reductions in the number of people suffering from tuberculosis or malaria.

Again, even when substantial adverse effects on welfare must be conceded, it may be possible to show that they were unnecessary incidents of the new undertakings by the government. Often one can point to such adverse effects having been detected and corrected in the past, without the new tasks having to be abandoned. One may be able to show that similar corrections can and will be made to eliminate the present disadvantages. The principle of argument remains, take up the alleged disadvantages one by one and either cancel them out or offset them.

In the nature of the case, better arguments cannot be expected; so to spurn these as inconclusive may seem idle. Yet they do not lay to rest all misgivings. Inattention to adverse effects in the short run aggravates uncertainty about adverse effects in the long run.

The politicians who put through new measures for government activity in promoting welfare have often not been alert to the disadvantages of the measures. They have not anticipated disadvantages; they have not moved promptly to remedy those that in time appear. Public support of higher education is a fine thing; sometimes, however, it means control of higher education by the lowest common denominator of state legislators. Strong welfare arguments favor government provisions for social security; but these provisions, on which citizens of all sorts come to depend, may be revoked in special cases from dislike of nonconformity, and under superpatriotic pressure.

Some real allowance, then, has to be made for adverse effects accompanying or following from active efforts on the part of governments to promote welfare. What should this allowance be? To suggest that the government renounce any active efforts evidently underrates the needs, short-run and long-run, to which those efforts respond. The best that can be done to limit government is to make as much as possible of alternative provisions, when these are not unduly costly; and keep a cautionary watch for disadvantages in measures that the government does take. The champions of limited government may find it congenial to address themselves to these points. So far as they address themselves perceptively, they deserve an attentive hearing from those who would otherwise feel no alarm about enlarging government.

2 / Evidence for Welfare
Shaped by Census-Notion

The subject of human welfare does not coincide with
the subject of rights, either by identity of meaning or
in relation, logical or empirical, to the particular practice of evaluating governments. In outlining this distinction, I have so far relied partly on the reader's
intuitive grasp of the meaning of the term "welfare"
and partly on an explicit list of some of the chief
aspects of the subject. I shall now proceed to the central business of this part of the book, which is to
characterize in appropriate detail the sort of evidence
that comparative judgments of welfare call for. This
characterization will further clarify the concept of
welfare and make even plainer its distinction from
rights and from other considerations.

Policies may be rejected and governments condemned by stringent use of the concept of welfare
under a perfectionist presupposition. As soon, for
example, as one person turns up whose condition ob-
servably deteriorates under a given policy, the policy
may be held to be disqualified either for approval
or for further consideration. However, the concept
of welfare typically enters evaluation under more
liberal auspices than those afforded by a perfectionist
presupposition. It is typically presupposed that because
of limited resources possibly all of the policies and all
of the governments to be dealt with are imperfect

ones; and hence that the aim of inquiry is to discover which of the policies or which of the governments is best compared with the others investigated. The nature of the evidence for a comparative judgment of this kind can best be appreciated by examining the form that the evidence will take when it is conclusive.

2.1. Census Form of Conclusive Evidence

This form, for each of the various aspects of welfare, is the form of a comparative census in which a certain property is to be looked for that will be found distributed among a given population.

Competent Observations Collected. By observing the condition and circumstances of any individual member of the population, a competent judge will be able to determine whether or not the member has that property. Members who have the property will be counted on one side of the census form for the whole population; members who do not, on the other. Furthermore, every member of the population must be accounted for. Either every member is to be observed, or on the basis of observing the members included in some reasonably accurate sample, inferences are to be made about the condition of members not observed.

The competent judges required need not in many cases be technical experts of any kind. They need only be people who can be relied on to make simple observations of familiar sorts. Such people can tell as well as experts that a child has no shoes; that a family sleeps on the sidewalk; that a certain village has never enjoyed modern medical services; that various people, more or less vehemently, dislike their jobs. Not all of these things, of course, can be found out in five seconds. It might, for example, take protracted observation of a man's attitude toward his job to establish the fact that uncomplaining though he might be he did not really find the job congenial. The investigation would still lie within the competence of ordinary men who have perhaps never taken a college course in psychology.

When experts have to be called in, they do not so much make ordinary observers superfluous as pick up where ordinary observers must leave off. Ordinary observers, for example, can establish well enough whether or not a farmer's crops have failed; whether his family is now skipping many of their customary meals; whether they are emaciated and listless. These are all observations of first-rate importance to the welfare consideration of nutrition. More refined observations, however, may call for expert knowledge. Only experts on nutrition could tell how much animal protein a man working at a certain rate needs, or what sorts of substitutions for this part of his diet might serve. But even in these judgments, the relevance of expert knowledge depends on connections with matters that experts are not needed to judge. If deficiencies in animal protein or substitutes did not result in emaciation, listlessness, susceptibility to infection, early death—matters open to ordinary observation— their claim to being considered in connection with nutrition as an aspect of welfare would vanish.

In principle, therefore, the evidence to be gathered in comparative censuses on aspects of welfare belongs to fields of observation in which ordinary citizens are competent to judge; or at any rate submits readily, through obvious implications, to check by evidence that does. When large populations have to be surveyed, it is true, sampling by statistical methods may turn out to be more convenient and sometimes (because of

problems in administering censuses) possibly more accurate than conducting complete censuses. Statistical
methods, though fairly widely known, do fall within
the special province of experts. The individual observations, however, do not. What statistical experts are
called upon to do is not to make individual observations, but to say how much information about the
whole population can be extracted from a collection of
individual observations regarding the members of a
sample. The resulting estimates—estimates as to the
proportion of the whole population provided for in
respect to some consideration of welfare or other—
must ultimately be vindicated by observations of the
same sorts as ordinary men could make, surveying the
sample; surveying further members of the population;
conducting complete censuses of the population as a
whole.

Arrangement in Comparative Census Form. Since the
various considerations arising under the concept of
welfare continually find expression in political discussion, and observations about the distribution of
connected conditions so largely remain within the
competence of rank-and-file discussants, one might
expect that the census form of evidence would be
familiar, indeed commonplace. I believe that it is,
though it has no familiar name. The name that I supply
for it—"the census"—is meant to strike a contrast with
its chief known rival, Bentham's proposed hedonistic
or felicific *calculus*. I hold that even for his own purposes of making innovations in ethics by reducing all
moral judgments to matters like welfare, Bentham
would have been better advised to rely on the notion of
a census than on the proposal for a calculus. The
felicific calculus, which was to measure the happiness

(positive) or unhappiness (negative) of every person affected by a policy and then reckon the algebraic sum (positive or negative) of happiness for the whole group affected, remains an unrealized project; whereas the census-notion has been in use for ages, wherever men have considered the effects of alternative policies on welfare.

The census-notion, in fact, figures very widely in comparative judgments about many sorts of groups and all sorts of distributive properties. The groups need not be composed of people. If one wants to know whether one shipment of apples is (on the whole) sounder than another shipment, one will ask what proportion of apples in the first shipment are sound—something that ordinary observers will have no trouble in telling—and what proportion of apples in the second shipment are; then compare the proportions:

	These Apples	*Those Apples*
Sound	80	50
Unsound	20	50.

On this evidence, the first shipment of apples must be said to be sounder than the second shipment.

Similarly, if one wants to know which of two groups of human beings is better nourished, one will in effect proceed to collect evidence for a comparative census:

	This Group	*That Group*
Properly Nourished	70	60
Ill-nourished	30	40.

These figures might represent proportions of the whole populations living under two different governments. If the difference in proportions could be ascribed to the policies (whether active or inactive) of the two governments, then the comparison set forth would strongly favor one government over another, as regards at least one aspect of welfare.

The census form may also be applied directly to the evaluation of different policies affecting the same population for example, to the future effects of two proposed policies regarding education:

	This Policy	*That Policy*
Finishing Eighth Grade	60	40
Dropping Out Earlier	40	60.

Assuming that it does conduce to welfare to have no less than an eighth-grade education, the comparison demonstrates that the first policy is better in this respect, from a welfare point of view.

These seem, of course, to be very simple matters; and I would like to stress the fact that very often they are quite as simple as they seem. Yet there are complications that must be faced and managed even at very primitive stages of using the census-notion.

Complication from Change of Persons. The most important of these is the complication that sometimes arises from a change of persons from one category in the census to another. Suppose that a nutritional census has been drawn up, comparing not the condition of different populations or of the same population under different future policies, but the present condition of a given population with its future condition under a proposed departure in policy. Suppose further that, so far as can be seen, the present policy could be continued if the government so chooses (and thus remains a relevant option). The results of the census might show proportions like those given before:

	Present Policy	New Departure
Properly Nourished	60	70
Ill-nourished	40	30.

It may seem that the results accord the same un-
ambiguous favor to one side of the comparison as
before. But this is not so, because of the possibility that
the people who will be ill-nourished under the new
policy will be, some or all of them, people who are
properly nourished under the present policy.

Sometimes such policies are chosen nevertheless. It
may be felt that the people losing by them have enjoyed unjust privileges. The fact that the losers would
naturally have preferred to go on with the former
policy will not be respected as an obstacle. Yet the
change of persons does present an insuperable obstacle
to inferring a comparative judgment about welfare that
is favorable to the new policy. If the new policy is
adopted, it will not be because it is favored on welfare
grounds alone.

The obstacle does not arise from the opposition of
preferences. If a change of persons did not occur—if
no one formerly properly nourished should fall after
the adoption of the new policy into the class of people
ill-nourished—many people's preferences might still be
opposed to the new policy. For example, many people
formerly able to stuff themselves might now have to
accept a more modest, though nutritionally adequate
diet. A welfare judgment could pass over this fact
without hesitation. Opposed preferences do not count
as an obstacle, then, when they occur among people
remaining within the same census category. When
opposed preferences occur as an incident of people
changing between categories, they do not count either;
a sufficient obstacle to a welfare inference is already

constituted by the fact that the evidence about welfare pulls two ways.

One might perhaps argue that the obstacle would be insuperable only so long as some hope remained of finding a more attractive alternative which did not have this drawback of worsening the condition of some members of the community. If this hope disappears, the fact must be faced that the people now properly nourished who will be ill-nourished under the new departure policy have perhaps no worse claim to welfare provisions than the people—40 per cent of the population, in the example—now ill-nourished who will be properly nourished under the new policy. Welfare alone cannot then be the decisive consideration; nor have I any intention of pretending that it could be. I am inclined to stress the cases in which welfare does give decisive guidance, in order to demonstrate its usefulness as a consideration; but I do not deny that its usefulness—like the usefulness of other evaluative concepts—is limited. It leaves many perplexities that may come up in politics unresolved.

In practice, I think, change of persons does not often force us to make such grim choices; I think, at any rate, that the concept of welfare and the use of the census-notion show the influence of assumptions that are in this respect optimistic. Presupposing normal opportunities for research and redesigning, comparative judgments of welfare are prepared to defer to evidence about change of persons. The deference amounts to suspending judgment while the proponents of new policies redesign them if they can.

2.2. Conflicts Between Census Topics

People who frankly accept the concept of welfare as a convoy concept, under which diverse considerations sail together, must face the further complication that these considerations sometimes conflict. Policies better as regards the supply of food may be worse, for example, as regards education or congenial employment. These different ingredients of welfare may then require to be weighed against one another.

Sometimes the difficulties of weighing do not present themselves. The improvements offered by a given policy all count from the beginning as net improvements. No person suffers losses in respect to welfare or any aspect of welfare; the provisions promote welfare in all its aspects simultaneously. Comparison, in such cases, may move quickly and smoothly toward pronouncing a conclusive evaluative judgment.

When the difficulties of weighing do operate they are often surmounted in practice by redesigning the alternatives considered in evaluation. Instead of accommodating the judgment to the complications of the comparison, the complications are eliminated so that a simple judgment is easy. What is it about the provisions in question that imply food can be increased only if congenial employment is sacrificed? Cannot the work be reorganized so that people do find it congenial, yet produce as much food? Often the provisions can be redesigned in some such way. Again conclusive judgments will be possible without requiring any weighing of the different ingredients of welfare.

Sometimes, however, the weighing cannot be avoided. Perhaps no one can conceive of alternative provisions that will increase food without sacrificing congenial employment. If policies are being compared, perhaps with the implication in mind that if the government follows the better policy it will be a better government, then a rational way of balancing diverse considerations is to balance them on an *ad hoc* basis, attending to the exigencies of the particular circumstances. A country desperately in need of food may reasonably choose to make large sacrifices of congenial employment, which a country fairly adequately supplied with food would reasonably choose to forego even at the cost of improvements in nutrition. If governments are being compared, then the government whose provisions for welfare best suit its *ad hoc* circumstances may be reckoned better.

There is a temptation in this subject to try for general solutions in advance of particular conflicts. Certainly it must be granted that it would be much tidier and more convenient to have the means for a general solution. Bentham was trying for such a means when he projected the felicific calculus. A calculus might serve if the different aspects of welfare could be systematically reduced in advance to a unique basis (like pleasure). The difficulty is that the concept of welfare, as we now understand it, does not have such a basis. Though there is no need to exaggerate the amount of possible conflict that the concept in its present condition is liable to generate, it is a fact that the particular aspects of welfare are not exhaustively enumerable. There is no standard list, but rather a great number of partly overlapping terms, which are subject to increase. Furthermore, the aspects are not so well coordinated that an exhaustive system of priorities, which would rule out any conflicts, can be discovered by analysis. To provide such a system of priorities by stipulation would beg particular policy questions, which the concept as it stands leaves open.

The present concept of welfare is in fact set up so as to leave particular conflicts to be settled in particular circumstances. It is in this respect (in contrast to the concept of rights) designedly *ad hoc* and advantageously so. To understand the concept, one must resist the natural desire for a tidy general solution. One must also resist what in this case leads to the same thing, the characteristic ambition of philosophical analysis to give complete analyses, which indicate in advance the truth-conditions for every application of the concepts analyzed. The concept of welfare turns out to be a sort of concept that does not admit of complete analysis in this sense. For the analysis to be complete, one would have to state in advance how all the particular considerations bearing upon the truth-conditions for the use of "welfare" are related, to the point of saying what follows for the affirmation or denial of general statements claiming improvements in welfare. Now, the various ingredients of welfare certainly form considerations bearing upon the truth-conditions for the use of the concept. But the co-ordination of these ingredients (e.g., of safety and morale) is left to particular circumstances (where, e.g., a relatively big improvement in morale may warrant some reduction in safety—or vice versa).

2.3. *A New Assessment of Utilitarianism*

These remarks have some significance for the assessment of utilitarianism—the misnamed ethics of human welfare. Controversies about utilitarianism have frequently revolved about the question whether happiness or pleasure (as reckoned by the felicific calculus, or by some other means) could be the sole ultimate criterion for good or evil. Many counterutilitarian arguments have taken the line that whether or not the calculus could be carried out, happiness could not be the sole criterion, because there were a number of other valuable things contributing to human well-being that might conflict with happiness or at least be desired in addition to it.

These arguments have succeeded far enough to make it a sensible precaution for utilitarianism to acknowledge the weight of the other considerations, even while their relation to happiness remains uncertain. But on neither side of the controversy have philosophers given much attention to the problem of how any of these considerations, happiness or the others in the convoy, apply in the absence of a calculus. It can hardly be maintained that these considerations do not get attention in practice; evidence about them provides familiar occasions for debate and investigation. In philosophy, too, their application has often been called for; yet a mystery has been left standing as to how their application is to be carried out.

The counterutilitarian arguments mentioned have the further defect of being slightly beside the point. Bentham's commitment to the project of the felicific calculus and the terms in which he concentrated attention on happiness as a matter to be reduced to algebraic sums of pleasures and pains warrant attack. But deeper attention to the topics being agitated would show that even for his own purposes it was a mistake for Bentham to concentrate upon happiness—just as it was a mistake for him to rely on the idea of the calculus. Bentham's practical purposes in policy-making—and the chief part of his purposes in ethical theory, where he was above all concerned to knock out

judgments opposed to human welfare and happiness—
could have been accomplished without using a supposedly comprehensive and completely analyzed standard, entirely fixed in advance. A convoy concept,
under which happiness sailed together with a number
of other considerations, would have served him better.
Once it was understood that all of these considerations
were used in conjunction with the census-notion, with
conflicts between different considerations (as demonstrated by censuses pointing in different directions)
to be settled *ad hoc*, the difficulties about how such
considerations were applied to policy would have been
cleared up as far as the facts of application could clear
them up. But the ordinary concept of "welfare" is
a convoy concept, and its familiar uses and relations
are in fact what vindicate the relevance of utilitarianism to choices of policy—and to evaluations of governments.

2.4. *Individualism of the Concept of Welfare*

Democrats, I am inclined to say, are on many topics
a species of utilitarian; but not all utilitarians are
necessarily democrats. A utilitarian, concerned with
welfare and scrupulous about evidence as to welfare,
might believe that popular government was in no
way the best means of accommodating policies to
such evidence. He could believe this without being
any less individualistic than those utilitarians who
undertake to act as advocates of democracy. For individualism is built into the concept of welfare along
with such scruples about evidence as the scruples about
change of persons.

In respect to individualism, in fact, the concept of
welfare does not in the end differ very much from

the concept of rights. Both can be used with the stringent sort of individualism that carries with it a perfectionist presupposition, though the concept of welfare is I think likely to be used this way relatively less often than the concept of rights. Both can be used without a perfectionist presupposition—in censuslike comparisons of two governments, both liable to be imperfect, or in comparisons of two expectably imperfect policies—though the concept of rights is I think likely to be used this way relatively less often than the concept of welfare. When it is so used, one compares proportions of the same or different populations whose rights—this right or that one, or a set—are maintained and respected; the census-notion applies in just the same way as it does to welfare considerations, when these are treated as matters for comparison between imperfect governments or imperfect policies.

Both rights and welfare remain individualistic in this treatment, in spite of the abandonment of a perfectionist presupposition. The benefits to be looked for under the heading of welfare break down, according to the census-notion, into benefits redounding to individual persons. On this point, in respect to welfare just as in respect to rights, modern Western democratic thought has taken a predominantly individualistic line. The notion of *group* rights—rights held and exercised by groups as such rather than by the members of groups (perhaps acting in concert)—has won for itself neither general nor persistent attention. Attention to group rights may have been thought superfluous, since groups are afforded a considerable amount of protection—perhaps all they would get anyway—by individual persons' rights to free association and assembly.

Separate attention to the welfare of groups—the myriad groups, large and small, formal and informal, in which people live and act and acquire their aims and characters—may likewise have seemed superfluous. Perhaps it seemed so with better reason. We can perhaps imagine what it would mean to speak of the welfare of a group as something different from the welfare of its members, though we would be mentally uncomfortable about a usage that permitted discrepancies of this sort to be asserted. In this usage, the welfare of a group would have to do with its survival and growth and power, all of which considerations might conflict with the welfare of its members. (At times their welfare might be best promoted by dissolving the group.) We would find it hard to imagine what incentive there could be for promoting the welfare of a group in ways that did not redound to the welfare of its members. But this difficulty is itself no doubt partly an effect of the individualistic bias of our traditions.

The assumption that the welfare of society and of all the groups that intermediately compose it reduces to the welfare of individual persons goes hand in hand with the doctrine that the welfare of individual persons is wholly determinable by some sort of observable evidence. The census-notion makes the relatively modest claim that census-takers can determine whether or not the individual people whom they observe fall into the categories of particular censuses. The project of the felicific calculus went further, to claim that it is possible to measure all the favorable effects together as the individual person's degree of happiness. Thus happiness substitutes for welfare. Economists— in spite of having given up hope of a felicific calculus —have been inclined to go further still, and to substitute preferences for happiness. They identify the provisions for welfare available in a given society with the total income there of consumption goods, and identify any case of a person's changing from consuming one bundle of goods and services to another bundle that he prefers as an increase in that person's welfare. Increase his income and (provided he acts rationally, according to his own preferences) his welfare—or something like his welfare—will increase, too, because he can now buy a preferred bundle.

Without trying to controvert the general assumption that the welfare of groups, like the welfare of society as a whole, is reducible to the welfare of individual persons, I would point out that this assumption, carried out with a very natural emphasis on consumers' goods rather than productive activity as the chief basis of welfare, has led to all sorts of unexpected and unpleasant difficulties. The clearest examples can be found in attempts at "scientific management" in industry. In these attempts workers' jobs have been redesigned so as (it was thought) to improve matters from everybody's point of view. By working more efficiently, sometimes with more productive machines, the worker would produce more, and increased output was a contribution to social welfare; but because he produced more, he could be paid more, and since his personal income would increase, the worker's own welfare would be advanced. Very often, however, redesigning the job left out of account the satisfactions that the worker got from his job under the former arrangements: satisfactions having to do partly with the status and privileges attached to the job, and partly (a connected matter) with the interactions—the reciprocal help and encouragement—in which he and a team or group of workers together participated. Increased income from the redesigned job could not make up for the loss of these things; and sometimes, I conjecture, neither the increased social output nor the increased personal income have been realized, because of the worker's resentful and noncooperative attitude.

Even if every ingredient of welfare is in the end assignable to individual persons, the ingredients that are necessarily associated with participating in groups tend to be less visible, less easily identifiable, than the ingredients not necessarily so associated—like income, or the bundles of goods and services bought with income. This difference perhaps suffices to explain the practical tendency for the individualistic approach to welfare to neglect the group ingredients. One way of correcting for this tendency might be to insist on separate (even if logically only preliminary) attention to considerations of group welfare. Something like this has indeed become commonplace in industrial management, though even here the magnitude of the opportunities for increased happiness and welfare that due attention to group life at work offers has hardly been recognized. If preliminary attention to the welfare of existing (and possible) groups would not suffice, or could not be counted on, perhaps more extended use of particular concepts of group rights would be in order. One difficulty, however, is that the groups which need to be protected on welfare grounds are often informal groups which might be made un- necessarily and sometimes obstructively permanent by granting them rights.

3 / *Welfare Distinguished*
from Preferences

The preceding discussion of the concept of human welfare, with its stress on the census-notion, has aimed at restoring certain simple commonplaces to their due position in discussions of political evaluation. I have held that the features of the concept of welfare required to make it testable are familiar, simple, and straightforward.

Plain and familiar as the concept of welfare seems to be, so analyzed, it represents a challenge to sophisticated treatments of welfare in which the census-notion has been ignored. There is current among economists, and not only among them, an impression that the ordinary concept of welfare, because it is evaluative, eludes definite tests. When they are working most rigorously at theorizing, economists incline to believe that the closest they can come to treating welfare is to redefine the subject in terms of preferences. They thus encourage themselves and others to accept the maxim that every man is the best judge of his own welfare, and the claim that welfare depends on preferences. Since preferences vary between persons, the welfare of a group of persons is best obtained by heeding their individual preferences.

The market, rather than the government, seems to be the suitable institution for doing this. The government at best adopts general rules approved by a majority of the people and requires the minority to accommodate themselves; whereas the market responds variously, with as nicely adjusted a variety as possible, to the different wishes of majority and minority— and of third or fourth or fifth parties as well. To judge a government's performance with respect to the welfare of the people living under it, therefore, one may be impelled to ask, at bottom, how much scope it allows for the expression of personal preferences and for their fulfillment; and to judge this by the scope that the government in question allows for market processes. (Thus the doctrine of limited government revives in its most sophisticated and appealing form.)

3.1. Conflation of Welfare with Preferences

Respect for Welfare as Respect for Preferences. A number of impressive lines of reasoning converge in support of conflating the subject of welfare with the subject of preferences. Some of them arise outside economic theory to reinforce those that arise within.

Among the considerations arising outside economic theory are these: It is certainly true that the happiness or welfare of any sane, normal adult will be diminished if he is not allowed to follow his own preferences in many matters. There are, in other words, some ingredients of welfare (taking welfare as a convoy concept) which depend upon the expression and satisfaction of preferences.

This scope for preferences—for freedom of choice —has compelling moral attractions of yet another order: for we think that the dignity of human persons requires respect for such freedom, and requires its exercise, too. (Otherwise a species of satisfaction that was obtained through drugs or through the electrical stimulation of the brain might suffice morally as a substitute for happiness.) Again, there is a famous thesis in philosophy—the thesis of Socrates that virtue is knowledge—which correctly reminds us of difficulties in conceiving of a person failing to choose what he firmly knows to be best for him and—perhaps not so correctly—encourages us to believe that given suitable information people can be counted on to make the right choices.

We might wonder, will right for them be right for all; but the present presupposition would be that in the market we are dealing not with controversies about what is morally right, but with the pursuit of happiness, given that a necessary minimum set of moral rules have been accepted and satisfied. We might wonder also whether the participants in the market do in fact have sufficient information to choose what is best for them; and this doubt cannot be easily laid to rest. The strongest answer that can be maintained at this point seems to be the hypothesis that imperfect as their information may be, individual participants do have some advantages in information over people other than themselves; and that these advantages can neither be compensated for nor realized through institutions other than the market.

Preferences in the Free Market: Laissez-Faire. The theory of the free market joins the argument here, bringing in its train the reasons inside economic theory for making welfare a matter of expressing and satisfying personal preferences. Myriad individual producers and myriad individual consumers meet in the market, each seeking to better his economic position, and each succeeding in doing so by exchanging things, including money, that he values relatively less for things, including money, that he values relatively more.

Given suitable information (again a big assumption) and freedom of access one to another, the process of exchange (and the process of production, which depends upon the former process once production is undertaken for the market) continues until no exchanges are possible that satisfy the fundamental condition for free exchange, namely, that both parties can become better off as a result. Without deliberate planning on the part of any superior authority—indeed without the individual participants perhaps needing to attend to any criterion for action besides their own self-interest—*everyone* participating is led by "an invisible hand" simultaneously to accommodate other people's preferences and to make the most of other people's willingness to accommodate his.

Charmed by this beautiful theory, which can be elaborated with many delicate refinements, people have often embraced the principle of *laissez-faire* without considering how difficult it is to test the theory or find circumstances in which the theory will fulfill its promises. A country poor in resources may remain poor whatever it does; the suggestion that it would have been poorer if it had not practiced *laissez-faire*, or richer if it had, will for want of relevant comparative observations in most cases remain only speculative. Other countries, if they do not differ in natural resources or geographical advantages, may differ so much in culture and social structure as to defeat empirical comparisons. On the other hand, scrupulous self-restraint on the part of a government surrounded by abundant resources will not vindicate the theory; it may have been a mistake to practice *laissez-faire*, but the costs of doing so may have been obliterated by the flow of resources.

The theory and the belief in *laissez-faire* that the

theory engenders rest on foundations remote from everyday affairs. The market that the theory envisages is a theoretically idealized market, characterized, for example, by perfect mobility and perfect information, by the absence of monopolies of any kind. If the case were conclusive for an idealized market, it would not be conclusive for a second-best approximation. In the real world of commerce, people are misinformed— often deliberately misinformed by advertising, a phenomenon that might not exist in the idealized market of theory. Their preferences are checked and confined in various ways by the exactions of monopolies. Furthermore, the disciple of *laissez-faire* must either ignore third-party costs (for example, the soot in the atmosphere, which neither the steelmaker nor the steelmaker's customer pays for); or concede that the government is properly called on to regulate or remedy in these connections, otherwise welfare will suffer.

Over time, these costs will mount up; they are likely to mount up especially rapidly during economic growth and technological change. But there is no guarantee that the market will arrange to remedy them, by evoking the production of remedial goods, much less eliminate the costs of bearing them or remedying them. Meanwhile, the costs may reach disastrous proportions. Cumulative effects may occur—in the course, say, of several generations, that hit welfare (or preferences) very hard, for example, by contaminating all the available supplies of water. These effects were never faced in the market, because the market, responding to short-run preferences for goods produced on the initiative of enterprises dependent on short-run profits, never made such effects matters of choice. Maximum solicitude for market preferences in each successive short-run period is unfortunately perfectly compatible with a decline over the whole sequence of periods in many aspects of achieved welfare, even reckoning these in relation to preferences.

Finally, neither the theory of the free market nor the principle of *laissez-faire* says anything about the distribution of property. Most believers have been content to have them say nothing. But if property is very unequally distributed (as it is in the United States and Canada) many, perhaps most people, making the same efforts as they would otherwise, will get more of the things that they prefer, or more of the things that they need, when the government takes active measures to compensate for the unequal distribution of property, say by redistributing part of the income going to property. There are counterarguments directed against this proposition, but they have a heavy burden of embarrassment to carry. For the market to operate fairly, everyone has to have a fair start; but disciples of *laissez-faire* must find it impossible to produce an historical record of a fair start ever having been made. One start would not be enough anyway. Every generation might well claim a chance to start anew. The argument against the claim is not that it is unfair, but that social arrangements would be calamitously upset by granting it, and that something can be done meanwhile to compensate for not granting it. Such an argument, moreover, requires both good faith and solid evidence, which are often not forthcoming, and sometimes may not be available. Would redistributing income or property worsen conditions in Sicily?

To these very serious reservations about the theory of the free market and its political applications, many others could be joined. Yet the reservations do not, even when combined, entirely destroy the economic arguments for treating welfare as a matter of preferences.

Indeed, while some economists have been busy enumerating these reservations, others have refined the theory of the free market in ways that heighten the attractions of treating welfare in this way.

Preferences Taken for Welfare Again: The Pareto Criterion. In a formulation that the theory of the free market used to receive from economists confident about the measurability of utility, the idealized market process was held to result in maximizing utility or satisfaction for the participants, taking these collectively and given their collective starting point in resources and skills. It would result likewise in maximizing utility or satisfaction for the participants taken individually, given their individual starting points in skills and possessions of marketable value.

Satisfaction in this connection had an obvious relation to preferences. People might be disappointed by what they expressed themselves as preferring beforehand; but they could not be said to be satisfied unless they obtained what they at present preferred.

Sophisticated modern versions of the theory of the free market move swiftly over the connection between satisfaction and preferences and start by burning the bridge behind them. They drop the notion of satisfaction, partly because it is not easy to conceive how to measure it, at any rate in ways that would validate interpersonal comparisons of utility, but chiefly perhaps because there turns out to be no need for economists to measure it in describing the operation of the market.

The theory runs more smoothly—no longer begging questions about measuring utility separately, or about satisfactions resulting from accommodating preferences—if it is stated wholly in terms of preferences. The process of exchange is now described as going on so long as a certain sort of discrepancy between different people's preferences persists—a discrepancy, namely, of the sort that makes it possible for all parties to an exchange to gain things that they prefer to have at the cost only of giving up things that their acquisitions are preferred to. The process comes to a halt when the market has reached what is called a Pareto optimum (after a celebrated Italian economist and sociologist active early in the present century): a position such that no one can become better off, in terms simply of heeding his own preferences, without someone else becoming, in terms of *his* preferences, worse off.

Associated with the notion of a Pareto optimum is the notion of the Pareto welfare criterion, according to which an action or policy will be said to "increase welfare" if it gives some people more of the things that they prefer without giving anyone less. An action or policy that thus increases welfare will represent a movement of the economy toward a Pareto optimum. Defects in the structure of the market, which block the economy from reaching a Pareto optimum or result in movements away from an optimum, will now be interpreted in terms of their effects on the expression and accommodation of preferences. Thus one need not depart from the subject of preferences in discussing either the virtues or the defects of *laissez-faire;* and all the reasons, inside and outside economics, for identifying the subject of welfare with the subject of preferences carry forward. It may be made to seem disrespect for the dignity of man and the freedom of the consumer to question the identification.

Pareto's guidance on welfare has, however, created very nearly as much confusion about the subject as Bentham's ideas about the felicific calculus. The two lines of thought are in fact connected: despair of realizing the felicific calculus motivated the retreat of sophisticated economists to the Pareto welfare criterion. The truth is that the Pareto criterion, like any criterion of welfare that takes only preferences into account, misrepresents the concept of welfare. The misrepresentation has of course not by any means frustrated all contemporary efforts by governments to make active provisions for welfare, beyond the scope of rights; but it has powerfully and illegitimately assisted the arguments of those who still incline to abide by the principle of *laissez-faire*. Just what governments can do for welfare, and can be expected to do by people evaluating them, will not become clear if the subject of welfare continues to be misrepresented as identical with the subject of preferences.

At bottom, welfare includes many matters, evidence as to which may run contrary to evidence as to the accommodation of preferences: food; safety; clothing; shelter; medical care; education; congenial employment; companionship. When evidence on these matters does conflict with evidence about preferences, evidence about preferences will be superseded, for it has at most a presumptive claim to being evidence about welfare. An economy in which a single rich maharajah held sway over millions of half-starved untouchables might have arrived at a Pareto optimum, so long as the maharajah did not care to change. But assuming that a redistribution of income could be carried out without the economy collapsing, it would have to be said that the economy was very far from doing as much as it could for the welfare of the people involved. Now, not only the peculiarly irrelevant stand of the Pareto welfare criterion would be overborne by the evidence in such a case (as would the felicific calculus as commonly understood). Even if the millions of half-starved untouchables sincerely expressed themselves as pre-

ferring a state of affairs that contributed so much to
the comfort of the maharajah and so little to their own
necessities, it would have to be said, again in the ordinary sense of "welfare," that their preferences notwithstanding, their welfare was not being served.

Economists working with the Pareto criterion do
not mean to deny that welfare in the ordinary sense
may not be served when the criterion is satisfied.
They would point out that in adopting the Pareto
criterion they were deliberately abstracting from the
distribution of property and income. (They are not
quite so clear or frank about departing from the
ordinary sense of "welfare," perhaps because they
have forgotten that even if everyone's preferences
were attended to, the observed results might not promote welfare.)

Deliberately it may have been; but deliberately does
not excuse them. For any contention about welfare
that they put forward using the Pareto criterion demands qualification—in big capital letters—to the effect that the distribution of property and income has
not been questioned. To be sure of preventing mis-
understanding, the qualification should really extend to
explaining how crucial an omission this is. If accommodating preferences is to be taken as tantamount to
promoting welfare, then at the very least one might
expect it to be stipulated that everyone's preferences
are to be counted fairly—which means, either equally
as between persons, or unequally only in ways consistent with variations in deservingness. Evidence about
welfare must be consistent with elementary considerations of social justice; otherwise it cannot be accepted,
as in the ordinary sense of "welfare" it is bound to
be accepted, as favoring an action, policy, or government.

3.2. *Preferences One Topic for Census Among Many*

Given the ordinary sense of "welfare" one properly resists the idea that even when fairly counted accommodating preferences is the same thing as promoting welfare. Yet among the distributive properties that may be surveyed by a comparative census is the property, to be determined separately for every individual person, of having real incomes—combined flows of goods and services—that they prefer to real incomes formerly obtained, whether or not their money incomes have changed. Suppose now that a comparative census of preferences is taken, respecting this property, and observing restrictions as to change of persons. Is this not equivalent to establishing whether or not the Pareto criterion of the economists is being approached or not being approached? If more people get what they prefer, without other people getting what they do not prefer, there is a movement toward a Pareto optimum. The test for having arrived at an optimum—or at least one test, which logically must be consistent with any others—is that no comparative census drawn up for the social state arrived at as against any other social state attainable from the present one would give conclusive results in respect to preferences indicating that an improvement was possible.

Application of the Pareto criterion may, in fact, be regarded as an application of the census-notion; but like the application of the census-notion to rights it is only one application among many. It is true that the Pareto criterion need not be bound to assessments of *market* preferences, or of purely *economic* policy;

it is essentially a perfectly general criterion so far as
the kind and scope of preferences at issue go. The
census-notion, on the other hand, operates freely over
all sorts of other topics besides preferences—topics
that, as aspects of welfare, may be more fundamental
than preferences and opposed to current manifesta-
tions of preference. Whether or not one wishes to act
on the difference, it is one thing to say that a policy
prohibiting the sale of cigarettes except in packages
labeled "poison" will conduce more to the welfare of
the people affected, by protecting their health better,
than the alternative policy—permitting cigarette manu-
facturers to suggest that their cigarettes are harmless.
It is quite a different thing to say that people prefer
one policy to another. People may in fact overwhelm-
ingly prefer the second policy. As confirmed smokers,
they may not wish to be reminded of the dangers of
smoking.

Another important advantage of the census-notion
in general over the particular application of it which
the Pareto criterion represents lies in the increased
facility with which its endorsement can be obtained
for *compensations*. The Pareto criterion itself is not so
rigid or so limiting as it may appear, since new possibilities of improvement sanctioned by the criterion
can be opened up by finding compensations for the
people who would otherwise lose out in terms of
their preferences. But these compensations must themselves suit the preferences of the people to be compensated: and people can be very stubborn about their
preferences, stubborn sometimes to the point of being
entirely irrational. Compensation under the general
auspices of the census-notion, on the other hand, need
be no more than compensation in kind: if a proposed
policy, which would bring great benefits in health to
a large proportion of the population, also endangers

the health of some other people, it may be redesigned
to include measures protecting the health of these
others. Compensation may also coordinate different
aspects of welfare. If in the course of procuring health
for many a policy endangers the employment of some
people, because, perhaps, it makes their skills obsolete,
then compensation might consist in provisions for
retraining and re-employment at comparable incomes.

The difference between the Pareto criterion respecting preferences and the census-notion applied to the
full range of welfare considerations represents a great
enlargement in scope for policy-making. It is true that
often a number of welfare considerations have to be
dealt with simultaneously, and balanced against one
another *ad hoc* when redesigning has failed to discover
a policy simultaneously superior in every aspect of
welfare. These are the complications of progress, however, not barriers to making any progress at all. Preferences, however, characteristically do tend to form
such barriers; and the effect of the Pareto criterion is
to accept this tendency without qualification, raising
opposed preferences—however few people have them
and however trivial they may be compared with
urgent needs for welfare provisions—into impregnable
barriers. In other words, the Pareto criterion surren-
ders almost all the arguments for welfare to the characteristic basis of opposition to social reforms of any
kind.

3.3. Influence of Preferences on the Concept of Welfare

The subject of preferences must be distinguished
emphatically from the subject of human welfare. Yet
it cannot be denied that the very meaning of the con-

cept of welfare, as well as its application to the evaluation of policies and governments, depends in various ways on preferences. What is congenial employment if it is not somehow consistent with a man's preferences? Yet people may seek employment or companionship on terms that reflect their preferences but do not in fact offer any objective prospect of satisfying their aims. They may not know what employment they will in the end find congenial, or what sort of company they will find companionable. On the other hand, they may in fact be satisfied with employment or with a species of companionship that fall far short of what could be provided for them. The fact that a man, lacking in experience or imagination, is satisfied with extraordinarily long hours and primitive conditions of work, or with having a few people to speak to daily who remember his name, does not imply that his welfare is being looked after. Preferences do not imply satisfaction; satisfaction does not imply welfare.

Logically, therefore, occasions may appear on which governments can promote welfare only if they override preferences; and in fact some social policies generally approved of by advocates of democracy aim at providing for people's welfare in spite of people's preferences to the contrary. Sometimes the people whose welfare will be provided for are the same people as those whose preferences will be overridden. At the very least, a democrat might want proof in such cases that the preferences of the people affected will change in favor of the policies after the consequences of these have been felt. But overriding people's preferences on the pretext of providing for their welfare can excuse all sorts of tyrannies, gross and petty. It is so dangerous to liberty and so objectionable to anyone who cherishes liberty that even a proof of the kind mentioned will seldom suffice. Generally speaking, once the difference between welfare and preferences has been made clear, advocates of democracy might well be inclined to respect preferences even when the preferences run counter to the evidence of welfare—as regards the same people. The scruples associated with the Pareto criterion are in this connection democratic scruples. However, even democrats ordinarily very scrupulous about attending to people's preferences do not always insist upon this condition. They do not insist upon it, for example, in the case of children, or in provisions for the insane. They will not tolerate a child's growing up entirely without benefit of schooling; they will have madmen restrained from cutting themselves up with knives.

Moreover, it is quite a different matter (though still so repugnant as to be avoided when it is morally possible to avoid doing so) to proceed against people's preferences when these run counter to other people's welfare. Social policies are frequently undertaken by modern governments, and approved by advocates of democracy evaluating those governments, which aim at providing for some people's welfare regardless of other people's preferences. The people opposed now, because the policies will reduce their comforts or undermine their status, may be expected to continue opposed. They may even become embittered opponents, with stronger preferences to the contrary, after the policies have been carried out. Their preferences will nonetheless not be given as much weight under most modern governments as considerations of welfare, at any rate when these are urgent. If a progressive income tax turns out to be a necessary means to financing a program for reducing infant mortality among the poor, then (other things being equal) the concept of welfare, as it is actually used to evaluate governments and policies, motivates the adoption of a progressive income tax.

Welfare Considerations Upheld and Weighted by Preferences. Preferences operate, of course, in giving welfare so much weight. If no one preferred—in politics—attending to welfare to attending to other people's preferences (even, for the most part, their own), governments as we know them would not be likely to override preferences opposed to welfare. But people do have a widely shared conception of welfare taking precedence over opposed preferences; and their preferences and actions give practical effect to this conception. Sometimes the welfare taking precedence is their own; but sometimes it is a third party's; sometimes it may even be the welfare of people opposed to the policy. It may be all these things at once: the health and safety of all members of the community may be increased by repairing gross omissions in the provisions for the health and safety of some.

Preferences also operate in giving different weights to the various considerations falling under the concept of welfare. There is something like a system for giving weights, varying with circumstances, which people learn to use along with learning the concept of welfare. If it does not mean waiting a week to eat, safety will be a more urgent consideration than food; in primitive circumstances, the initial weight given to food will be greater than the initial weight given to education. The marginal weights given to any of these considerations change, however, when the needs regarded as most urgent have been provided for. Long before everything has been done to assure every member of the community of a healthful diet, resources will be diverted to education. These weights are effective as a consequence of preferences; but, again, people do have a widely shared conception of how the weights differ and change; and their preferences and actions give practical effect to their conception.

I say, something like a system for giving weights. The likeness encourages economists to speculate about comprehensive social welfare functions, which, given these weights for defined circumstances, would rank every combination of social policies therein proposed. The failures in likeness indicate that the weights will not be forthcoming to the extent that such functions would require. Most of the decisions that have to be made about marginal weights have yet to be made; and they will, in the normal course of events, be made only as they become necessary—*ad hoc* in particular choices, not between comprehensive combinations of social policies, but between incremental features of one or two immediately at issue.

Nevertheless, the concept of welfare and associated notions of weighting are sufficiently firmly established to exculpate people who put welfare ahead of other people's preferences from the charge of merely making an invidious distinction in favor of their own preferences. The suggestion that there is nothing but an invidious basis for making such a distinction simply begs the question whether all preferences are to be treated on the same footing. In fact, widely shared moral convictions concede preferences according with welfare precedence over opposed preferences. The concession covers a person's own welfare.

Naturally, some cases are clearer than others; if what a person wishes to provide for is not an urgent welfare consideration in the circumstances, or perhaps a prime consideration respecting welfare in any circumstances, his arguments may not be thought morally compelling. The concession may also be abused; a person may pretend that his welfare has been endangered in order to gain undeserved advantages. Numbers of other cases remain in which a man, even when expressing a preference for promoting his own welfare, will have the support of moral arguments that justify overriding other people's preferences.

Preferences Reflected in Scope of Welfare. There is a further connection between preferences and the concept of welfare which deserves attention. Not only, given the concept of welfare with its present content and applications, must it be said that the concept would not have practical effect if people's preferences did not operate accordingly. It must also be recognized that the concept would not have its present content and applications if people's preferences had not operated in distinctive ways to shape its development. Welfare is a concept for community use in generating and justifying policies; but people will accept it as such only if it reflects preferences that they have in common. A community of ascetic flagellants would marshal very different considerations under the heading of "welfare," at least in respect to life in this world, from the considerations marshaled under that heading in contemporary North American society. There are occasional variations even among contemporary North Americans. Amish people, for example, do not give education the same important place among welfare considerations that the society surrounding them accepts without question. The Amish believe that too much education unsettles religion and undermines their way of life; and they prefer keeping up their religion and way of life to prolonging the education of their children.

Much is obscure about the ways in which preferences operate in the development of concepts. It is dif-

ficult, for example, to disentangle the effects of preferences from the effects of beliefs. Like the Amish,
flagellants no doubt have certain beliefs which help
explain their practices. They may believe, for instance,
that the pleasures of this world are one and all temp-
tations of the devil. Is it their beliefs or their preferences that chiefly affect their conception of welfare?
But in connections like these beliefs and preferences
are likely to be mutually adapting; it may be impossible to identify either as the original source of influence.

The fact that neither beliefs nor preferences may be
fully articulate aggravates the difficulty of sorting out
their effects. One can sometimes point to explicit trains
of reasoning, set forth in legislative debate, executive
proclamations, or judicial opinions, which indicate that
the concept of welfare is being extended, and make
clear what sorts of preferences are calling for the extension. Arguments for ending the practice of segre-
gation in schools and other public facilities have given
indications and clarifications of this kind. Yet even
these arguments fail to make entirely clear the sort of
connection that desegregation has with welfare. Is
desegregation henceforth to be treated as a primary
welfare consideration, itself an ingredient of welfare,
or is it to be conceived as only a means to serving
primary welfare considerations? An option like this,
which affects the definition of the ordinary language
term "welfare," is not the sort of thing that is settled
by explicit debate. It is resolved by the long-run operation of custom—by thousands of small shifts in linguistic usage. Likewise, the modifications in preferences that in the long run will lead, we may hope, to
segregationists themselves or their descendants re-
linquishing their present position will not proceed by
explicit announcements. The expression of preferences

in debates about welfare, and the conscious adoption of successive policies because they seem to be dictated by certain considerations assimilated to welfare, give only occasional glimpses of broader processes of conceptual change.

Another option, equally basic, and continually, like the option about means or ingredients, recurring as the concept of welfare undergoes pressure for development, lies between treating various considerations as matters of welfare—means or ingredients—or leaving them outside as matters to be disposed of by preferences, however frivolous. (Again, it is an option for the most part resolved obscurely in ways not fully articulate.)

For example, a person might well prefer having a varied diet, with a good deal of meat and leafy vegetables, to eating nothing but rice and beans. Other things being equal, other people might sympathize with such preferences and do something to advance them. They would not, just by doing this, be committing themselves to treating a varied diet as a matter of welfare. Yet provisions for a varied diet do now have a secure place among welfare considerations. As conventional notions of minimum subsistence have changed, in fortunate countries at any rate, so have the standards for achieving nutrition as an aspect of welfare.

The options of assimilating new considerations to welfare extend not only to enlargements of established considerations but also to establishing radically new considerations. The subject of education was once such a novelty. The subject of congenial employment may still be one for many people. People do not, of course, fail to see the attractions of congenial employment; but they may not consider it is a matter to be dealt with under the heading of welfare. At best, they may think

of congenial employment as a sort of gratuitous amen-
ity, which only especially fortunate people can expect
to enjoy. Often, in our society, people ignore the
whole subject, concentrating their attention upon the
amenities to be enjoyed outside of working hours.

These amenities—television programs; sports facilities; national parks—conventionally fall outside the
concept of welfare at the present time. They figure,
of course, as subjects of public policy. Their attractions, extolled in political arguments, motivate social
decisions. They are, however, by and large still things
that people consider they may or may not do anything about, as they please. Yet the position of these
subjects may already be changing. Is it not sometimes
contended that mental health requires access to open
spaces in nature? Certainly physical health often comes
forward as an argument for sports facilities (sometimes, I wager, as an argument for facilities devoted
to spectator sports). If these arguments displace others
in gaining a hearing, the considerations in question
will change from being merely amenities open to
preference to being in the common view indispensable
features of a tolerable life. The option will have been
exercised to make them matters of welfare rather than
of preference.

Once the option has been exercised in this way, the
matters in question call for evidence about the observable condition of people affected one way or another
by the different policies being judged, or the different
governments being evaluated. As we have seen, this
evidence is liable to be very different from evidence
about preferences, and sometimes directly contrary in
its tendency toward a favorable or unfavorable judgment.

3.4. The Definition of Human Welfare

How much has the preceding discussion accomplished toward the definition of "human welfare"? The discussion did not begin with a definition, and it would have been unnecessarily restrictive to require one at the beginning. Very often, a philosophical discussion must search for a definition that no one knows how to produce straight off. The discussion of rights, however, did produce, very soon after it got underway, a formula for defining the concept of rights. One might reasonably expect the discussion of welfare to offer something equivalent before it is brought to an end. I shall offer something equivalent simply by summing up briefly what I think the preceding discussion has established about the concept of welfare.

Welfare, according to the results achieved in this discussion, is something different from rights; and also something different from preferences. Like either of these concepts, the concept of welfare may be used in a perfectionist way, with a stringent individualism ready to condemn a government or policy as soon as one case of deficiency is discovered. But it is most often used on the assumption that the issue in hand requires a comparative judgment of different governments or different policies, both of which may be imperfect. When it is applied, under the auspices of such an assumption, the conclusive form of evidence sought is the form of a comparative census. Comparative censuses may also be made respecting rights and preferences. The difference from welfare at this point lies in the more extensive variety of particular considerations that press for attention under the heading of welfare.

The variety of considerations has been illustrated by mentioning food; safety; clothing; shelter; medical care; education; congenial employment; companionship. This list, however, is not especially privileged as to the categories mentioned; nor is it complete. "Welfare" is a convoy concept under which an indefinite number of particular considerations, even now increasing in variety, may be marshaled. Now, these particular considerations may conflict with each other on occasion; but it is a mistake to try to settle such conflicts in advance by taking them into account in the definition of welfare. All one can say is that the conflicts will be settled *ad hoc*, according to marginal differences in accommodating various considerations in particular circumstances. But it is important and illuminating to say this; it gives further light as to just what sort of concept the concept of welfare happens to be.

3.5. *A Comprehensive Test of Welfare*

I shall now bring my discussion of human welfare to an end by outlining a comprehensive test of welfare embracing many different aspects.

Important as the *ad hoc* adjustments are that are called for in applying the concept of human welfare to the evaluation of policies and governments, allowing for them need not prevent advocates of democracy from settling upon an intelligible comprehensive test. Such a test, I suggest, would cover the categories of our familiar list: food; safety; clothing; shelter; medical care; education; congenial employment; companionship. For each category, the provisions made by the government now existing most successful (according to the evidence of a comparative census) in its policies respecting the given ingredient of welfare may be taken as defining the minimum standard of performance (at least for governments with the same or greater resources). Perhaps agreement might be obtained, for one or more category, on a higher standard; for it might be demonstrated that no government now did as much to provide a certain ingredient of welfare as it could. A standard based on the actual best performance—the performance of Sweden or Switzerland, say, in nutrition; or of Great Britain in medical care for the whole population—would serve, however, and perhaps serve very well, not least because it could not be criticized for being impractically idealistic. Countries with smaller *per capita* resources might be excused in various degrees for inferior performances respecting welfare, by considering how far their resources fell short of those available to the government whose performance was taken as standard.

Resources must be understood very broadly, to include such things as rainfall and other benefits of geographical position; and cultural differences, such as the presence or absence of a large class of vigorous entrepreneurs. The test leaves room for doubting whether successful performance always follows from active organization of these resources on the part of the government. Where it does not the government deserves credit, which the test will give it, for its self-restraint.

I shall not define the test with the further precision that would enable it to discriminate between the overall performances of two governments one of which fell below the defined standards in some categories yet met others, while the other government met the first but failed the second. Such a comparison would either require the *ad hoc* adjustments to be expected in particular cases of comparison on the subject of welfare; or would presuppose arriving in advance at a system for weighting the different categories. I doubt whether advocates of democracy are currently prepared to agree to such a system, or would be wise to be so prepared. As it stands, the present test is capable, like the test of rights, of comparing governments with tolerably good performances all around and governments with comprehensively bad performances; or governments that match in every respect except that one performs badly in one category where the other performed well enough to pass. I believe that the test is in consequence capable of application to a number of important questions.

Advocates of democracy bring forward as means of evaluating governments not only the concept of rights and the concept of welfare, but also the concept of collective preference. They ask that governments provide for and promote welfare, consistently with respecting and maintaining rights; they want both these tests passed in ways that reflect the preferences of the people whom the governments serve.

Concern for rights and concern for welfare characterize advocates of democracy, as figuring prominently among the tests which they apply to governments; but (as has been pointed out before) neither of these concerns distinguishes democrats from nondemocrats. Either of the concepts, rights or welfare, may be taken up by nondemocrats; either may be handled in ways that democrats would not relish. Insisting upon the rights of a privileged minority may obstruct provisions for the welfare of the majority. On the other hand, some rulers or propagandists may be ready, waiving any scruples about rights or about change of persons, to promote welfare simply in terms of overall statistics.

Concern that expressions of collective preference determine policy is (alone among the three evaluative tests that we are considering) distinctive of advocates of democracy. Again, this test may be at odds with the others, and not only because the others may be championed by nondemocrats, or democrats without scruples. Democrats, too, may find themselves pulled in different directions by indications from the test of rights, from the test of welfare, and from the test of collective preference. Concern with all three tests is a necessary condition of being accounted a democrat. Passing all three tests is a necessary condition of a government's being accounted fully acceptable in a democrat's eyes. Hence if any one of the three tests is failed, the government in question will fall short of being what advocates of democracy ask for. What distinguishes them from other evaluators is that besides being concerned with rights and welfare, they wish and expect to reconcile these subjects with the further concern with collective preference. (In details, to be sure, they are often concerned with rights and welfare in ways that nondemocrats might not accept.)

At last, with this concern with collective preference, the subject of preferences comes into its own as an ingredient of democratic evaluations. In the preceding discussion, preferences took second place. Rights (once acknowledged, then invoked) obviously override them; and welfare, too, though it is not a subject to be identified with rights, differs from the subject of preferences. Preferences, it was conceded, play a part in enlarging the range of particular considerations falling within the convoy concept of welfare. Once this part has been played, and new considerations are accepted into the convoy, they logically require independent treatment, however. Objective observations must be made that may conflict even with the expressed preferences of the people observed, let alone the expressed preferences of other people.

1 / *Direct Tests*

1.1. *Basic Connection with Majority Rule*

The tests respecting collective preference that advocates of democracy use have something to do with majority rule. The problem is to see just what. Any satisfactory test for majority rule, as we shall shortly see, will have to carry with it a complex of conditions; and even when these conditions are satisfied, the simplest tests fail to cover numbers of important cases, e.g., cases in which representative rather than direct democracy is being practiced. I shall begin, however, with relatively simple tests—"direct tests," as I shall call them, because they are general enough to apply to direct democracies as well as to representative ones. Later I shall use the conditions worked out for these as the basis for constructing an "indirect test," which will by design apply to representative democracies only.

I would prove that the tests have something to do with majority rule in this way: Consider a community of sane adults for which a number of mutually exclusive policies P_1, P_2, P_3 . . . P_n have been proposed. Suppose that it is known that a majority of the members of the community prefer P_3 to all of the other policies—that is to say, it is known that with one vote each to cast they would vote for P_3. (I shall throughout this part use "prefer" in this broad technical sense, standard in economics and the theory of voting. ("Prefer" in the ordinary sense has a much more limited range; we do not have mere preferences for living or dying, though we might have votes to cast or other choices to make.) Nevertheless, the policy adopted for the community is not P_3, but (say) P_2.

I hold that advocates of democracy would find this result objectionable. I do not say that given further information they might not be reconciled to the result nevertheless; but I do say that further information would be needed. As it stands, it is a flagrantly undemocratic result, and as such to be condemned unless it can be specially explained and justified.

A further inference can be drawn from the example, at least tentatively. It is the inference that the tests that advocates of democracy wish to impose respecting collective preference are more fundamentally concerned with relating collective preferences to policies than with relating them to the choice of representatives or rulers. (Without undermining the inference, the choice of these might be regarded as special cases of adopting policies.) Moreover, though the example given might be said to be just one example, in this respect insufficient to support inference to such a general thesis, it happens to be as an example peculiarly abstract and generalized in content. If it works at all— if it is (as I hold) sufficiently significant to be repudiated as flagrantly undemocratic—it may well work also to support the inference about policies being more important than representatives or rulers. Nothing is assumed in the example about representatives or rulers; they may have been elected by the most elaborate of the many elaborate provisions that current governments make for popular elections. Nevertheless, if there is a policy that the majority favor and it is not adopted, the result is flagrantly undemocratic.

In what follows I shall subordinate procedures for choosing representatives or rulers to procedures for choosing policies. I shall take it that what advocates of democracy look for ultimately, in matters of collective preference, is the fulfillment of certain conditions respecting the adoption of policies, and among these conditions there somehow figures a desired relation between policies and majority rule.

To bring this relation to light, I shall begin by describing a paradigm of adopting a policy by majority rule; I shall attach to the paradigm a set of conditions each necessary and together sufficient to make it, for advocates of democracy, beyond argument a satisfactory manifestation of collective preference. Then I shall stretch the paradigm into a test of a government, by adding further conditions. A government, of course, deals with a range of policies and has to be tested with reference to its procedures of adopting policies throughout this range; it could not be evaluated from just one instance, however paradigmatic. Afterward, I shall depart from the paradigm and modify the stringency of the test in various ways, to reach other, more practical tests of collective preference; but I shall try to retain enough of the attractions of this first test to make the others convincing.

1.2. Majority Mandate: A Paradigm

Consider again a community of sane adults for which a number of mutually exclusive policies $P_1, P_2, P_3 \ldots P_n$ belonging to the same issue (in a sense to be explained) have been proposed. Suppose that the policies are put to a vote, all the policies being offered simultaneously and the voters being instructed each to cast a single vote for one policy. A majority ($\frac{n}{2} + 1$, or $\frac{n + 1}{2}$, depending on whether n is even or odd) or more of those voting (n) cast their votes for P_3. What now must we lay down as conditions for this incident to be a paradigm of what advocates of democracy demand respecting collective preference?

Adoption Condition. Recalling the flagrantly undemocratic result of the previous example, no doubt the first condition that springs to mind is a condition about adoption: policy P_3 must actually be adopted and (so far as feasible) carried out. What constitutes adopting or carrying out will characteristically vary as between kinds of policies. Putting a law on the books that may never need to be enforced is, for example, a very different matter from constructing a system of dams for flood control. I shall not inquire into such differences. All I want to say about the adoption condition is, first, that though communities that conduct votes of the kind described generally do provide for the adoption condition, the provisions may be imperfect; for example, the officials who have conducted the referendum may dislike the result and delay heeding it so long that carrying out the policy becomes impossible. But, second, so long as those who are responsible for carrying out the policy—permanent officials or *ad hoc* ones—do so, it does not matter logically to fulfilling the adoption condition how those officials are chosen. They might be hereditary monarchs; or representatives of the people duly elected for brief terms by universal suffrage. Either might serve, just as either might obstruct.

. . .

Participation Condition. To be assured that the vote for P_3 and its subsequent adoption really was a manifestation of democracy, advocates of democracy would demand some assurances about participation. Some of these assurances would have to do with the quality of participation. I shall sum them up by stipulating that every voter must understand what his vote will signify in this instance, namely, that if it is joined by a sufficient proportion of the other votes, the policy that he has designated will win; that there must be no intimidation of voters—every voter must be free to cast his vote in accordance with his own unintimidated preferences; and that voters are not to be bribed.

Other assurances would be required respecting the proportion of participants in the community. The easiest course to take, if a paradigm of majority rule is wanted, is to demand that every member of the community (every sane adult) cast a vote; but this demand appears to be excessive. Countries have been accepted as democratic in which women were excluded from voting; and countries where rates of participation approach 100 per cent have not had this fact taken as evidence of democratic practices.

If advocates of democracy will accept countries that exclude women from the franchise as democratic, what they require in this part of the participation condition would, I think, be this: that the members of the community who are eligible to vote shall be drawn as near as possible in the same proportions from every major geographical section and major social stratum of the community; that those drawn from every given section or stratum shall be sufficiently numerous and randomly distributed to be statistically representative of the distribution of preferences within that section or stratum on the issue between P_1, P_2, P_3 . . . etc.; and that those eligible to vote shall actually vote in sufficient numbers so that a majority of those voting will also be a majority (though possibly a smaller proportion) of all those eligible to vote.

These three points may seem too precise and abstruse to be ascribed to advocates of democracy generally; but I do not think they really are too precise or abstruse. If democrats will accept men voting while women do not, would they not accept an arrangement under which only heads of households voted? The fact that every section and stratum was drawn on in the same proportions would at least save the arrangement from being categorically disqualified. The representativeness in a statistical sense of the sample of eligible voters drawn from each section or stratum has a reasonably firm foundation in the distaste which advocates of democracy feel for highly biased samples (élites, vested interests)—a distaste which they could feel, of course, without using statistical terms to express it. The final point, about a majority of those voting having to be a majority of those eligible to vote, might be less stringently put if one could be sure that advocates of democracy would be satisfied with less; but here I think the evidence points the other way, toward stringency. Common outcries indicate it conflicts with democratic expectations to have a small turnout of voters and a large body of stay-at-homes. So it is thought elections should not be so numerous or frivolous to deter people from casting votes, though it is expected that for one reason or another even in the most crucial elections not everybody will be able to get to the polls.

Genuine Alternatives. It is important, in the eyes of advocates of democracy, that among the policies put to a vote, there should have been at least one genuine alternative to the winning policy P_3. The assumption that the policies at issue were mutually exclusive assists in defining this condition, but does not go far enough.

By "mutually exclusive" in this connection, it seems sensible to mean not that there is no compatibility between the features of one policy and the features of others, but simply that each policy has at least one feature that is incompatible with some feature or other of any given policy belonging to the set. So P_2 may be identical with P_3, except that P_3 has some added feature that P_2 does not, for example, undertakes certain disbursements or projects of construction that P_2 does not; we shall count them as mutually exclusive policies.

Each policy belonging to an issue will thus consist of a number of features F_1, F_2, F_3, etc. But, taken pair by pair, every policy will differ from every other one in at least the presence or absence of some given feature; and it is understood that if one policy is adopted, none of the others will be, though features that any of these have in common with the adopted policy will be accepted. I now define an issue as a disjunction of policies—P_1 or P_2 or P_3 or . . . P_n—that are mutually exclusive, have actually been proposed, and have been brought forward simultaneously for voting.

By being mutually exclusive, the policies belonging to the issue voted upon in our present paradigm are guaranteed to be different in more than formulation. I do not think that we have begged any important question in furnishing this guarantee. It is true differences in formulation may elicit different responses from voters in the way of expressed preferences, but advocates of democracy would not, I believe, grant that P_2 and P_3 were genuine alternatives if their formulations were logically equivalent. If voters did not recognize the equivalence, they would be deceived. If the system did not count a majority of votes split between P_2 and P_3 as prescribing the same policy as a majority for either P_2 or P_3, there would be something wrong with the system.

The differences between P_2 and P_3 may, however, seem trivial even if they do not consist merely in differences of formulation. Imagine that the community in which the vote is taken is ruled by a dictator, who has divided his henchmen into two carefully matched groups; he has designated one group the "Blues" and the other group the "Greens." P_2 then is identical with P_3, we may suppose, except that P_2 (the construction of a network of military highways, say) is to be carried out by the Blues, while P_3 (the construction of the same highways) is to be carried out by the Greens. Or imagine that the only difference between P_2 and P_3 is that if it is adopted, a description of P_3 is to be printed in green ink, rather than blue.

In the face of such examples, one may well be tempted to stipulate that to count as genuine alternatives, P_2 and P_3 must differ in their effects upon the rights or welfare of (some at least of) the members of the community. I think, however, that this temptation should be resisted. It seems to me injudicious not to allow for voters' preferences between alternatives on any grounds whatever, supposing that the alternatives are logically distinct and mutually exclusive, as explained above. They may have important grounds for preference that we do not anticipate (e.g., they may prefer to alternate between favor for the Blues and favor for the Greens; or to concentrate favor upon the Greens, in the hope of arousing envy among the Blues). But whether the grounds are important or not, the fact that voters do have preferences between alternatives should be enough (in this respect) to qualify the alternatives as genuine, given that they are logically distinct.

For P_i (any other policy) to qualify as a genuine alternative to P_3, then, P_3 and P_i, besides being mutually exclusive, must be substantially different in this way: some at least of the voters must prefer P_3 to P_i. But here the test for preferring cannot simply be the fact that some of them vote for P_3 rather than P_i; for we already know that; we now want to know what it signifies. I suggest that the test depend on eliciting a weak ordering of the policies proposed from each of the voters, namely an ordering in which the voters may rank any policy above any other as preferred, or two or more policies on the same level as matters of indifference relatively to one another. The present part of the condition as to genuine alternatives would imply that in the orderings offered by some at least of the voters P_3 would be ranked, not on the same level with P_i, but ahead of it.

How many of the voters must be ready to supply such orderings? It seems inadequate to require that only one of them be ready, even on the supposition that the rest would vote at random; for a majority so composed would not *have* a majority preference in the full sense required, and a policy carried by such a majority could not be said to reflect majority desires or wishes or sentiments. If a majority of those voting supplied such orderings, we would have grounds (though perhaps not conclusive grounds) for saying all these things. But some relation must be stipulated between this majority and the majority required under the participation condition. Otherwise it would be possible for the latter majority—which will carry the day—to be composed of a minority with such orderings—a minority both of those voting and of those eligible to vote—together with a number of indifferent voters (who have voted at random). Not all of those who rank P_3 ahead of P_i will necessarily rank it ahead of every other policy proposed; some may vote without voting with the majority. To guarantee P_i's being a genuine alternative to P_3 in the eyes of those who carry the day for P_3, we must say, a majority of those voting for P_3 no less in number than a majority of those eligible to vote shall rank P_3 ahead of P_i. This requirement allows for a number of those actually voting for P_3 to be indifferent as between P_3 and P_i, which is at least a gesture toward realism; the larger P_3's majority in proportion to the number of those eligible to vote, the more largely it may be composed of indifferent voters.

We have in effect now allowed that P_3 and P_i may be genuine alternatives without differing in what appear to us to be important respects; and the main reason for making this allowance consists in scruples about imposing our sense of what is important on the voters. Our allowance goes far enough, however, to let P_i be a genuine alternative even when the voters themselves feel the difference from P_3 is trivial—so long as the required orderings are available. Should the present test take precautions against the alternatives voted upon being only trivially different?

If there are only trivial differences among the policy proposals belonging to the issue, the issue may reflect complacency on the part of the community, and this complacency may be well-founded in the sense that there is in fact no urgent need to deal with the issue, and therefore not much need to worry about how it is disposed of. On the other hand, the limitation to trivial differences may betray a dangerous lack of imagination on the part of voters and their leaders; they really have no grounds for complacency. But there seems to be no reason to forestall this eventuality, much less the other, in our paradigm. Democracies are not to be made imaginative by definition. If the differences are trivial, and in being trivial, signify no more than complacency or lack of imagination, the paradigm will still work out to a democratic result.

Trivial differences and poverty of alternatives may, however, signify something more serious, against which the paradigm must be protected. The poverty of alternatives may result from artificial, counter-democratic manipulation. A clever dictator might offer the voters alternatives from time to time and make much of his readiness to heed majority will. Yet he could carefully suppress from the agenda any alternative that he himself disliked. To rule out such artificial manipulation, let us say that every policy or proposed policy reaching a vote shall have been "effectively proposed"; that any group amounting to some small proportion of the community, large enough to prevent abuse by cranks (or dictators) and small enough to be easily mobilized, may effectively propose any policy it likes; and that every effectively proposed policy reaches a vote. The genuineness of the alternatives will thus depend in a natural enough way on their having escaped counterdemocratic preselection.

The condition about genuine alternatives must, finally, require not only that there must be in the set of policies proposed at least one genuine alternative to P_3 but also that if this alternative had received a majority (like the majority received by P_3, qualifying under the several conditions being examined) it would have been adopted and carried out (so far as feasible) instead of P_3. The adoption condition does not guarantee that this would happen, for it does not discriminate between a case in which P_3 happens to accord with the sentiments of a dictator (who would not in fact tolerate any other policy) and a case in which a dictator was not on the scene. Advocates of democracy would, of course, most earnestly want to discriminate between such cases.

Is an Information Condition Needed? All the conditions so far defined might be satisfied without the result of adopting policy P_3 being agreeable to advocates of democracy. For P_3—in contrast to some genuine alternative present in the set of proposed policies—might affect the rights or welfare even of those who voted for it relatively adversely; or it might turn out once adopted, to accord less well with the preferences even of these voters. Mistakes of this kind are (one is inclined to suppose) frequent in politics; and the ignorance that leads to them is embarrassingly widespread. Policies are frequently (and often deliberately) misdescribed to the voters; but they may be widely misunderstood even if they are described quite truthfully. Can a result brought about by ignorance and confusion be the sort of thing advocates of democracy want to issue from majority rule?

Of course it is not; but the question is whether (if it satisfies other conditions) such a result is to be treated as not an instance of majority rule at all, or as an instance of majority rule gone wrong. Some points about information have been implied already, in laying down the previous conditions: According to the participation condition, the voter must know what the effect of his voting in this instance will be, if his vote is joined by a sufficient proportion of other votes; according to the condition of genuine alternatives, the proposals must differ in more than formulation, and on the basis of this difference voters (in sufficient numbers, as stipulated) must be prepared to supply weak orderings of the policies. We may suppose (if it is not taken as implied, we further stipulate) that those offering such orderings understand what ordering involves. Since the orderings are made on the basis of the policies as mutually exclusively described, no question of their being misdescribed in their very formulation arises. The voters may be deceived about what policies their representatives or rulers actually intend to carry out; but if there is a discrepancy of this kind between the policies proposed and the policy or policies actually to be carried out, either the adoption condition or the condition of genuine alternatives will be violated.

Having the sort of information required by these points leaves plenty of room for majority rule going wrong. But do not advocates of democracy leave this room themselves? Do they not envisage the possibility —many kinds of possibility—of a majority of voters making mistakes? Surely they do envisage such possibilities; they do not assume that majority rule is attainable only on condition that it operate perfectly. But to go further in requiring voters to be informed would mean arbitrarily excluding some practical and familiar possibility of voters being mistaken. If we say, policies shall not be misdescribed by having false consequences attributed to them, we in effect surrender the chances of there being a practical instance of majority rule in any serious empirical matter; for the imperfections of human knowledge are such as to make misdescription of this kind inevitable. If we say, the voters shall not misunderstand the bearing of the policies as proposed on their rights or welfare or future preferences, we are requiring a perfection of information that even experts cannot have.

There is, moreover, something invidious in laying down further information conditions. For who is to tell the majority that it is misinformed? Experts are fallible; on important political questions, experts generally disagree. They cannot expect to override those that they have not convinced. In the glorious words of William Jennings Bryan, "The people have a right to make their own mistakes." These words are, of course, perfectly consistent with efforts to provide voters with more information, drawing on expert knowledge; but we need to distinguish between the conditions needed for democracy to work well and the conditions implicit in determining that something is a democracy.

Must it not at least be stipulated that the voters be informed that such and such policies have been proposed and that a vote will be taken on them at such and such a time and place? Minimum but perhaps sufficient requirements along these lines have in fact already been laid down in stating the participation condition and the condition of genuine alternatives. A majority of those voting is required to be a majority of those eligible to vote; and a majority of those voting for the winning policy no less in number than a majority of those eligible to vote must order the winning policy ahead of at least one of the alternatives to it, though they may be indifferent as between all the rest. A majority of those eligible to vote therefore have enough information not only to turn out but also to rank the winning policy ahead of the others. They may be mistaken in so ranking it, but in the end that cannot be helped. If other voters have not turned out because they were not informed, their turning out would make no difference to the result.

If it fulfills the adoption condition, the participation condition, and the condition of genuine alternatives, the vote described, which results in a majority for P_3, supplies a popular mandate for that policy. The conditions are each necessary and together sufficient to make the incident a paradigm of majority rule, as conceived by advocates of democracy. Now we must consider how the paradigm is to be incorporated into a test respecting collective preference that is applicable to governments.

1.3. Majority Mandate: The Test

Governments are continuing institutions, which deal over time with a variety of policies. To be accepted as democratic, they must do more than adopt from time to time a policy with paradigmatic majority support; they must continually meet a test of some sort regarding the range of policies that they pursue. Advocates of democracy would wish to say that the whole range of policies pursued by a government must have obtained majority support. Maybe this will turn out to be too much to ask for, so that advocates of democracy will sensibly settle for less. But evidently to have the whole range supported in this way would gladden a democrat's heart; it would enable the government to pass democratic tests respecting collective preference with flying colors. What would it mean to have the whole range supported?

Describing a Range of Policies.   There is a preliminary difficulty to be coped with about how to describe a whole range of policies. What a government does over time is susceptible of being described in many different ways, and the range of its policies will look different according to the mode of description employed. One might say of a given government, "It has a policy of promoting the general welfare," and claim that this description covered everything that the government did. One might also say, "It has a policy of appointing bachelors as well as married men to high diplomatic posts . . . a policy of requiring farmers to take land out of cultivation if they are to receive subsidies . . . a policy of naming aircraft carriers after revolutionary battles. . . ." and so on, operating at a level of such minute detail that it looks as if one will never get to the end of describing all the policies in the range.

I doubt whether there is any elegant way out of this difficulty. The way out that I propose to take is to relate the range of policies to some institutional basis and call for the judgment of a selected committee of citizens or observers. One such basis, for the United States, might be the organs of government described in the Constitution, together with the principal agencies created since (say, all agencies the heads of which are appointed with the advice and consent of the United States Senate). I assume a committee large enough to be representative of a range of opinions embracing 90 per cent of the population eligible to vote and small enough to deliberate reasonably efficiently. This committee is to be asked to list what it judges to be the most important policies pursued by each organ and agency—the one to six most important policies, say, depending on the size of the organ or agency's budget. Policies of not doing something— not providing outdoor relief for the able-bodied un-employed, for example—are to be included, if they are deemed sufficiently important, as well as active policies. I suppose (in accordance with everyday ob-servations) that members of the committee can agree on what is an important policy even when they have diametrically opposed views as to whether it should or should not be supported; but we may allow in case of disagreement about importance for a minority of the committee to add one or two policies to the list in the majority report.

To simplify dealing with the committee's report, we may require that it so formulate its report as to list only policies logically independent of other policies in the list, in this sense: any given policy could fail to be pursued and all the others nevertheless remain in force. When we speak of a policy being put to a vote against various alternatives, we shall further suppose that all those alternatives are logically independent of any other policy on the list and of the alternatives to that policy. With the given policy, the issue that they form is a logically independent sphere of mutually exclusive policies.

Other ways of generating a serviceably complete description of a whole range of policies might easily be imagined. I claim for the method just described only that it shows some way exists which accords at least in a rough and ready way with democratic sentiment.

Sweep-Through Condition. Given a serviceably complete description of the range of policies pursued by a government under test, what test is the government to meet respecting this range?

It may be suggested that the test should consist in the capacity of every policy in the range to receive a mandate fulfilling the conditions of the paradigm. There is no doubt that this fact, if it were a fact and were known to be a fact, would be thoroughly convincing. The trouble is that passing such a test can be so much more easily asserted than established. If (as we may expect) the greater part of the range of policies were covered only by conditionals depending on very indirect and inconclusive evidence—of the form, "if P_3 were put to a vote, it would receive a mandate"—the test would be no better than a journalist's hunches. In this suggested form, the test, indeed, might be answered and passed by conditionals alone.

The opposite tack would be to demand present evidence of a mandate for every policy. With up-to-date technology, one can even imagine meeting this demand. Suppose that every voter has at home an electronic panel on which every policy taken into account by the given serviceable description is represented by an on-or-off switch; next to this switch, in each case, are switches for all the genuine alternatives that have been proposed for the policy. (If there are in any case very many of these alternatives, some rule might have to be found for limiting the number represented; but for the moment let us suppose that there is no need for such a rule.) All the home panels are connected with a master panel in the capital, which automatically registers the existence of a mandate as I have defined it. With this system one could tell at a glance whether there was any policy that did not have a present mandate. As soon as a sufficient number of voters changed the settings on their home panels, the mandate registered for a certain policy would disappear on the master panel; perhaps a new mandate would appear for one of its rivals.

The searching present test of collective preference that such an electronic system would make possible could hardly be said to fall short of democratic expectations. I think the main trouble with it for our purposes is that it outruns them. Paradoxically, it resorts more fully and immediately to voting than advocates of democracy have hitherto contracted for. Such advocates might quite properly have serious reservations about the electronic system. Democratic demands respecting collective preference have often been accompanied by important presuppositions about prior discussion of issues. The discussion, it has been supposed, would be long enough for people on various sides of the issue to present their arguments to the public; sufficiently audible and visible for every eligible voter to have a reasonable chance to come across these arguments; and sufficiently focused, in respect to any given issue, to show how far the various arguments answered to one another. These are all matters difficult to realize in a fully satisfactory way, and advocates of democracy may not have dared to claim assured enlightenment for every voter; but they have expected that there would be time to publish information about policies and ventilate issues before votes were taken.

Such expectations would be more easily fulfilled by taking up policies one by one, focusing attention on different issues turn by turn, rather than presenting the whole panel of issues simultaneously. I shall seize upon this clue and define the test in which the paradigm is to be incorporated in this way: a government will pass the test only if the whole range of policies that it pursues (under a given serviceably complete description) is swept through within some relatively short period of time and every policy either receives a mandate or is replaced by one that does. The optimum time might vary between six years and twenty-five, depending in part at least (and inversely) on the rapidity of general social change; let us for present purposes stipulate twelve years.

To soften the impact of certain technical difficulties connected with pairwise voting on more than a pair of proposals, I shall suppose that when a policy is voted upon during the test period, all the alternatives to it effectively proposed during the period are presented to the voters, together with the given policy. One might say either that no more alternatives happen to be proposed after the vote or that the vote just happens not to be taken until all the alternatives of the period have been proposed.

Reassortment Condition. Something more must be said about the provision of mandates over time before the present test will have been defined to the full satisfaction of advocates of democracy. The need for a further condition may be seen by reflecting on the possibility that mandates may be continually forthcoming as debate sweeps through the whole range of policies—but always from the same people. Consistently with the mandate test as so far defined, the community living under a given government may be divided into a majority of voters who always have their way and a minority who never do. I believe that advocates of democracy would object to this situation. Their conception of collective preference commits them not to majority rule *per se*, but only to majority rule so far as this can be reconciled on the one hand with the possibility of unanimity and on the other hand with the existence of diversity. (Even then, as we have seen, they are prepared to consider that majority rule may lead to mistakes in policy.)

All democrats, I believe, have some feeling for unanimity. They are inclined to think that at least as regards some fundamental issues—like the issue of whether there shall be one government in a given territory—unanimity is desirable. On such issues, they might think, majority rule is misused if it does not point toward unanimity, but instead deepens and exacerbates conflicts. Some would think that if majority rule on any issue is going to divide the community radically and permanently, it would be best not to bring the issue to a vote in the first place—to exclude it from politics. (A particular argument for limited government then emerges: government should be limited as much as possible to noninflammable issues. Sometimes the argument will not work for enough people; a vote will be insisted on in spite of its dangers.)

Advocates of democracy drawn as I have supposed them drawn from English-speaking countries would also favor diversity; and so would their allies from other "Western" democracies. They would not relish seeing a majority consistently victimize a minority; somehow, diversity should be capable of surviving (unless it is the sort of diversity that endangers the rights and welfare of the community as a whole). But how can this be provided for in matters that are brought into politics and put to a vote without renouncing majority rule in favor of at least occasional rule by minorities?

The way to do it is (in part) to make sure that as one mandate succeeds another one, the majorities and minorities involved go through a process of reassortment, so that ideally no one would be in the minority in all questions. I shall therefore associate with the mandate test a condition about reassortment, to the following effect: no voter shall be in the minority in more than 90 per cent of the mandates exhibited during the period of the test; and each of 90 per cent of the voters shall be in the majority in at least one-third of the mandates exhibited. The condition could be satisfied by a series of unanimous votes on different issues; but it allows also for the much more likely possibility that there will be no issue on which the voters are unanimous. The figures stipulated in the condition are, of course, arbitrary to a degree; they may be regarded as stand-ins for the actual figures that would be settled on *ad hoc* by people employing the mandate test in any actual instance. By "voter" here, one might understand "person eligible to vote." I think, since a strong condition as to participation has already been imposed, it will suffice to take the present condition in the weaker sense of applying to people who actually vote at least once during the test period.

In practice, minorities might appear whose preferences would not seem to deserve the application of the reassortment condition. Imagine, for example, a faction, amounting to 12 per cent of the voters, each of whom supports only policies which violate personal rights or diminish human welfare. Would any of these people deserve to win once, let alone one-third of the time? Allowing (as we allow) that such policies may be proposed, surely we would not want to commit ourselves to having some of them adopted. The attractions of the reassortment condition or of any particular proportions stipulated for it will vary with circumstances, more than the attractions of other conditions. It is not being proposed as something that advocates of democracy will infallibly commit themselves to; but only as something that will increase the attractions of the test if it can be applied without adverse results. For present purposes, I am assuming that adverse results do not appear; vicious minorities either do not exist or have been rendered ineligible to vote.

The majority mandate test is now before us. It consists of a paradigm of what a majority mandate is, plus further conditions for applying the principles embodied in the paradigm to a government and hence to a range of policies. It is to be applied over a twelve-year period to the whole range of policies pursued by a government under test, on the understanding that the reassortment condition is to be met during this application. I hold that if a government passed this test, advocates of democracy would accept it as performing satisfactorily respecting collective preference (even if it performed less than satisfactorily in other ways, e.g., in maintaining rights or in promoting welfare). There are possibly other tests that advocates of democracy would accept in lieu of this one—we shall look at some other tests in a moment. At this point it is important to agree that however that might be, this one is an acceptable test. I shall introduce the other tests as weakened versions of this one.

Let it be recalled that the test will apply to representative governments as well as to direct ones. By passing the test, a representative government would demonstrate that its institutions, however complicated and indirect, are set up so as to suitably reflect collective preference in the policies they pursue.

Practical Application of Majority Mandate Test. How practical is the test? I began by thinking, as I started to work it out, that it would prove to be very impractical; but now that it has been worked out, I am not sure that this is so. I conjecture there may be a chance that relatively to some serviceably complete descriptions some governments in the real world would actually pass the test, provided that the votes required were taken. Moreover, if the serviceably complete descriptions in question were (as they might be) reasonably broad and simple, I think that it would be practical to carry the mandate test out. The procedures, observations, and deductions required would not be impossibly burdensome.

On the other hand, it seems likely that a critic could produce, for any government in the real world, a short list of detailed policies being pursued by that government that could not easily be accommodated in applying the mandate test. Any serviceably complete description of policies that the policies on the list would figure in (or be implied by) would not be especially broad or simple. To match the details of the policies on the short challenge-list, the serviceably complete description would have to descend to great detail throughout all or most of its range; and hence it would tend to embrace a great number of issues and require a great number of votes. The government might still be capable of passing the mandate test; but it would be so difficult to find out whether it did as to be practically impossible to know. The community might not have time to take all the votes required; or it might have time for nothing else.

The fact that the test can be passed (or failed) only relatively to some given serviceably complete description of the whole range of policies swept through may be felt to be a difficulty. Could not a government pass relatively to one such description and fail relatively to others? My discussion has not been precise enough to prepare us to evaluate this possibility. Perhaps I can help reduce alarm about it by pointing out that by definition a serviceably complete description of the range of policies will be anchored to the institutions of the community, during the inspection of policies carried out by the representative committee that is to produce the description. Hence there are limits on the variation in serviceably complete descriptions alternative to any given one; all the serviceably complete descriptions produced for a given community will tend to resemble one another. Moreover, the mandates observed during the period of test will be offered for policies as actually formulated when put to the vote. For the test to be carried out, these policies must correspond to policies listed in the serviceably complete description used in the test; and the necessity of this correspondence puts another limit on variation in the relevant alternative descriptions. The relevant alternative descriptions will have to include the same or corresponding policies; and in respect to these a government that passes the test for a given list of policies does not seem also liable to fail it. The hypothesis that it might fail the test for some other set of policies, not actually put to the vote, may be an idle speculation in many or most cases.

The Special Case of a Majority of Minorities. For all that has been said hitherto about the nature of the policies for which mandates are to be supplied, they might all be policies each of which affected every voter in the same way, with the same mixture of advantages and disadvantages. Voters might still differ, of course, in their preferences as regards the mixture of advantages and disadvantages offered by any given policy and the mixtures offered by the alternatives to it. They might differ in the degree to which they applied self-regarding or other-regarding considerations to the choice between policies; or, so far as they considered only their own self-interest, they might differ in the value that they placed on any given advantage or disadvantage, for example, an increase or decrease in educational facilities. Nevertheless, looked at in this way, the policies pursued by a government can naturally be thought of as adopted because each of them does something for every member of the community (whether or not given members welcome its being done for them).

The policies pursued by a government may sometimes, however, invite quite a different sort of description. As regards objective advantages and disadvantages (provisions for welfare or backing for rights) they may each offer benefits to some group or groups of voters and to others either no benefits or concrete drawbacks like taxes. Looked at and described in this way, moreover, none of the policies enumerated may benefit a majority of voters (or a majority of those actually voting); every one of them may do no more than serve a minority without regard to the majority or even at its expense.

With a suitable description and enumeration of policies, a similar result may be obtained even for a range of policies each of which objectively benefits every voter in the community. For voters may differ so much regarding their preferences for each of these policies that none of the policies commands majority support; each of them is supported by no more than a minority of the voters.

Yet in both cases the government that pursues the policies may satisfy the mandate paradigm even if it does not pass the mandate test. We have supposed, in constructing the mandate test, that policies on different subjects would be put to the vote separately, issue by issue; and though I have not defined precisely what is to be counted as a difference in subjects (nor, in abstraction from concrete examples, do I intend to), it seems contrary to the spirit of the mandate test in the form supplied to envisage combining policies on different subjects and putting them to a vote together. It is nevertheless important to see that the mandate paradigm may reasonably embrace such cases; I shall draw upon this fact in my further constructions.

Minorities in favor of policies on different subjects may combine (with or without overlapping) in support of all the policies taken together, and a majority so formed, a majority of minorities, may perfectly well offer a mandate of the paradigmatic kind. The case is important, moreover, not merely because it indicates that the reach of the mandate paradigm may be wider than at first appears; but chiefly because it shows that a government may perfectly well devote itself to serving minorities, each according to their own interests or preferences, without ceasing to conform to majority rule (or, for that matter, at the extreme, to unanimity). A democratic government may on this ground justify subsidizing shipyards, maintaining tariffs on textiles, supporting farm prices, or even catering to the refined tastes of very small minorities. The Canadian Broadcasting Corporation, for example, which is paid for by the Canadian government, broadcasts some programs of chamber music, though it hardly gives them as much time as it gives programs about ice hockey.

Ultimate Lack of Realism in the Majority Mandate Test. In spite of all the precautions taken in setting it forth, the mandate test remains highly unrealistic in the sense that there is (so far as I know) no country in which popular voting upon policies is carried on extensively enough for the test to be answered. There is, furthermore, no realistic prospect of any country's changing over to provisions for extensive popular voting of the sort required. Even countries in a position to pass the test, if there are any, are not going to change over. Now, one could say without further ado that countries which do not provide for so much voting on issues are countries which cannot be shown to be democracies. But this would be a mistake, because there are alternative tests respecting collective preference that would be acceptable to advocates of democracy in lieu of the mandate test. On examination, some of these may be adaptable to the complications raised in representative democracies by the practice of taking popular votes on candidates rather than on policies.

1.4. A Bargaining Test

Among the alternative tests that deserve examination there are a number of direct tests. Some of them would carry as much conviction as the majority mandate test: for example, a test differing from the mandate test chiefly in substituting for the single ballot a scheme for rank voting, which would score $(n - 1)$ points for the policy that a given voter ranks first, $(n - 2)$ for the policy that he ranks second, . . . and finally 0 points for the policy that he ranks nth. The policy with the largest aggregate number of points, summed for all voters, would win. Or one might consider a test with runoff provisions, which would have similar effects in opening up room for voters' preferences—other than their first-place preferences—to count. The results of voting, under schemes meeting these tests, might differ from results accepted by the mandate test; sometimes the winning policy would not have a majority of first rankings behind it. But the results would not be less acceptable, I think, to advocates of democracy. If a majority of first rankings existed, it would win.

I shall pass over alternative tests relatively close in spirit to the mandate test and move immediately to examine a test relatively distant from it, though still, I believe, within the limits of being persuasive to advocates of democracy. This is a test in which, again, policies win adoption when majorities support them; other policies emerge from a process of bargaining. Instead of adoption by mandates, or as well as adoption by them, adoption as a result of applying the weighted voting scheme to given issues may take place; but again, it is supposed that a number of policies are adopted as a result of bargaining, without being voted upon at all.

Let us consider a government that for any reasonable stipulated period of time fulfills the following conditions: (1) It receives majority mandates during the period for some at least of its policies. (2) It affords reasonable opportunities for any of the policies that it pursues, under some serviceably complete description of the range of these policies, to be called up for a vote, at which mandates alone would decide the issue. (3) During the period it adopts *new* policies other than those voted on only after conducting a bargaining process open to participation on the same terms of eligibility as exist for voting. We suppose that these terms of eligibility satisfy the participation condition. We suppose, in fact, that in any instance of voting, the participation condition as a whole is satisfied, and also the adoption condition and the condition of genuine alternatives.

Would such a government be accepted as democratic by advocates of democracy? More to the point, can we add conditions that would ensure its acceptance, without sacrificing the increased realism which this test seems to promise?

Voting Part of the Bargaining Test. The sweep-through condition lapses by explicit abdication in the formulation of the present test; but the concern behind it may still be honored in part. Without requiring that the whole range of policies actually be voted upon, one may now require that the whole range be susceptible to voting so that doubts about a policy's being popularly supported can be quickly resolved. If the range is to be susceptible, it should be easy to have any policy in it voted upon. No doubt it would be impractical to allow any voter, acting alone, or any very small number of voters to call up a policy. But the "reasonable opportunities," mentioned in the second defining feature of the present test, for calling up a policy and voting upon it might be such as, for example, to enable 1 per cent of the voters to call up a policy by petition and effectively propose any alternative to it they like. 1 per cent may be too high or too low, depending on the size and complexion of the community in question.

If one asks for reasonable opportunities to call up policies for a vote, is there any point in asking in addition that some policies actually be put to a vote during the test period? The entire absence of instances of voting, however, would raise grave doubts about whether reasonable opportunities for calling up policies did in fact exist. 1 per cent may look fine on paper, but in a large, very mixed, and widely scattered population be practically impossible for petitioners to round up. The absence of voting would, moreover, raise doubts (of a kind that we have not encountered before) about whether the population was sufficiently active politically for their government to be reckoned a democracy. A population in which not even so many as a reasonable number of petitioners ever takes a sufficient interest in any policy (or alternative to a policy) to call for a vote would be too sluggish or apathetic to suit advocates of democracy. (We need not consider seriously the possibility that the population is perfectly happy with all the policies pursued or ignored by the government.) Furthermore, for the voters to be aware of their opportunities and knowledgeable about how to use them it may be essential that the opportunities be seized now and then and voting actually practiced.

So the present test does well to require that some policies at least win backing in votes taken during the test period. Shall we attempt to specify which policies, or how many? There is perhaps a temptation to say that they should include the most important policies, which might be held to be those that affect rights and welfare most substantially. It is far from clear, however, that issues respecting rights and welfare will be better settled by votes than by bargaining. If those concerned prefer to settle them by bargaining, it seems reasonable to respect this preference.

I am more inclined to attempt specifying how *many* policies are to be included among those actually winning in votes, even though the specification is bound to be very arbitrary.

There is some difficulty about fixing on a proportion: to require 50 per cent of the range of policies to be voted upon seems too much, as 10 per cent seems too little; perhaps we could agree on 20 per cent as a figure capable of satisfying advocates of democracy. There is another difficulty. The serviceably complete description that we invoke to define the whole range of policies pursued by the government under test must be sufficiently rich and detailed to list an acceptably large number of policies. The smallest number of policies for which a proportion of no more than 20 per cent can be exhibited is five. Will it be enough for one of the five policies ascribed to a government to be put to a vote and win? I conjecture that it might be enough, small though it looks. Given reasonable opportunities to call up policies for a vote, and other things being equal, we might sensibly stipulate that relatively to a serviceably complete description distinguishing at least five policies, at least 20 per cent of the policies pursued by the government shall win in votes during the test period. Both numbers would be arbitrary. Our consolation would have to be the fact that they would not be entirely arbitrary, any more than the notions of "big proportion" or "little proportion" are entirely arbitrary; and the fact that we do not need to discover optimally reasonable numbers, just numbers that will satisfy.

However, before five becomes the stipulated minimum number of policies to be furnished by a serviceably complete description—at least one of them to be put to a vote and win during the test period—the reassortment condition needs to be looked at. Insisting that some number of policies actually win backing in votes opens up a way for the bargaining test to satisfy an analogue of the original reassortment condition. For (assuming that simple majority voting is used when the votes are taken) one may require (first clause) that no voter shall be in the minority in more than 90 per cent of the mandates exhibited during the period of the test; and (second clause) that each of 90 per cent of the voters shall be in the majority in at least one-third of the mandates exhibited. Indeed, no word of the original condition need be changed, though now it must be understood that some number of policies escape the condition by not being put to a vote at all.

But this new understanding of course makes a radical difference in applying the condition. If reassortment as now conceived is to be plausible it must have some chance to operate. Not one out of five, but at least three out of as many as fifteen policies must be put to a vote if the second clause is to be satisfied without being satisfied in excess—which in effect would make the condition more stringent than intended. For the first clause to be satisfied without being satisfied in excess, at least ten policies out of as many as fifty must be voted on and win. Ten policies are not enough, however, to assure voters normally in a minority of any variety of winning policies. No minority would be guaranteed to be on the winning side in more than one of the ten. I think that to begin to give a persuasive chance of variety, something like fifty policies—10 per cent of an even larger number—would have to be voted upon during the test period. Then every minority would be part of a majority on at least five policies. Accordingly, the stipulation regarding the number of policies that are to win in votes during the test period may be revised to read: relatively to a serviceably complete description distinguishing at least 250 policies, at least 20 per cent of the policies pursued by the government shall win in votes. Two hundred fifty is a big jump from five, and perhaps an astonishing place to land—why just there? It offers itself not as an ideal number, or as a uniquely suitable one, but only as one that would satisfy the demands of advocates of democracy if it were obtained. Even so, the stipulation does not guarantee that the five policies falling to the lot of the most consistently outvoted minority will embrace matters very important to them. But the original reassortment condition does not offer such a guarantee either. To make sure of minimum defenses on some matters important to minorities, I am supposing that advocates of democracy would insist upon the tests of rights and welfare.

I have now shown how to reconcile the voting part of the bargaining test with the conditions that ensure the acceptability of the direct test of collective preference previously considered. The bargaining part of the test remains to be examined.

Bargaining Part of the Bargaining Test. Bargaining would have to take care of all the new policies adopted during the test period without actually being put to a vote. (Policies brought into question and then continued, after a favorable vote or after bargaining, may count as new ones.)

On a broad view, making it easy to imagine how the bargaining allowed for might occur in a direct democracy, which I continue to have chiefly, though not exclusively, in mind, these policies might embrace all sorts of matters on which the administrative officials of the government remain inactive, though the policies are ascribed to the government nevertheless. Various contracts entered into by businessmen, for example, the creation of new business firms, or the distribution of corporation profits, would be reckoned as particular policies of the government, because they were particular consequences of a general policy of *laissez-faire*. In a direct democracy, qualifying as such by the bargaining test, voters might have all sorts of time to discuss such matters apart from the occasions now and then on which political meetings occurred and votes were taken. Apart from such occasions, on matters not then dealt with, they would make whatever arrangements suited them by striking one bargain after another with different assortments of people.

To count all these arrangements as official policies of the government, however, would paradoxically make it difficult to describe the government as a limited one even when it was in fact practicing *laissez-faire* so punctiliously as to keep its own activities within very stringent limits. To escape the paradox, we might consider the activities of government to be limited to what administrative officials do; to policies actually adopted by the electorate in votes; and (making room for governmental policies originating in bargaining) to policies officially brought to the attention of the electorate without being challenged or repudiated. Suppose, in a direct democracy, that the voters meet and transact some public business by discussion followed by voting; then without leaving the place of meeting, they break up into small groups and bargain over such matters as how various neighborhoods are to be policed. Before the day ends, the meeting is again called to order; at this time spokesmen for the different groups announce to the whole body of voters the results of the bargaining, e.g., "In our neighborhood, down by the water, we're going to carry on the police work by rotation among the heads of households." The chairman calls for comments; but whatever comments arise do not happen to lead to any further votes being taken. The meeting breaks up with the understanding that the announced results of bargaining are henceforth official policies of the government, which all citizens are bound to respect.

May it not be objected that in this illustration the announced results of bargaining have in effect won unanimous consent? No doubt in some circumstances unanimous consent would be implied; but the acceptability of the bargaining test does not depend on its being implied. The circumstances might be such that those voters who opposed the results were either too small a number to arrange for a vote or too small to hope to win, and hence unready to press the issue. Or, whatever their number, they might think the issue not worth the trouble putting it to a vote would cause. Instead of understanding that the results had won unanimous consent, the participants might infer no more than that the results had not been opposed with sufficient determination to reach a vote. The cogency of the test in relation to voting lies in its effective provision for recourse to voting, when recourse is urgently desired, rather than in substituting unanimous though tacit consent when voting does not occur.

The example of police work shows that functions

ascribed to even a very limited government may be arranged for through bargaining. In applying the bargaining test to a direct democracy, one might insist that certain functions be ascribed to the government and covered by the test. Furthermore, whatever one's objections in principle to the government's assuming certain other functions, one might accept it that they had in fact been assumed from the attention given them in official proceedings. In the illustration, they would include all matters on which results were announced to the whole meeting, after the bargaining had taken place and before the meeting broke up.

A community might practice direct democracy and still (as we have allowed) have administrative officials to carry out the policies directly voted for. Bargaining might take place between officials and individual citizens, or small groups of them. It might in fact go on continually, on the occasions now and then occurring for meetings with votes and announcements, and in the intervals between such occasions. In a representative democracy, there will be bargaining of this kind with the continuing bureaucracy. There in addition will be bargaining between voters and their representatives, among the representatives, and between the representatives and the bureaucracy. It is easy enough to relate the results of bargaining in these new dimensions to the government as policies that the government pursues, since one can connect them with decisions and activities on the part of the officials. But what shall the bargaining test, which as a direct test (on my definition of a direct test) is to apply both to direct democracies and to representative governments, require about bargaining in these dimensions?

The third defining feature of the bargaining test stipulates that the government shall adopt new policies (other than those backed by votes) only after conducting a bargaining process open to participation on the same terms of eligibility as exist for voting and that these terms shall satisfy the participation condition. However, being open to participation might mean no more than being given a chance to attract the attention of other possible bargainers. This chance would not be worth much to citizens who lacked information about the new policies that the government might be contemplating or about the times and places of hearings. So the third feature should extend to requiring that the government publicize the new policies it is contemplating, and the times and places of hearings, by means reasonably calculated to make the information available to all people eligible to vote. Just what these means would be would vary considerably with circumstances. One might suppose that announcements in official gazettes would rarely suffice, whereas preemption of all prime time on television for blanket coverage would in most circumstances be unnecessary.

Besides being open to participation far enough to give every citizen a chance to speak, the bargaining process might be asked to give everyone who speaks a chance of being listened to and even accommodated, in bargains from which he receives something he subjectively values relatively more in return for giving up something he subjectively values relatively less. At any rate, let us say, the bargaining process should be such that everyone could enter it and strike a number of bargains such that overall he gains by the bargaining process. One might add that he should gain more than he would by calling for a vote on the policies at issue. There are, however, many difficulties in the way of understanding exactly what these conditions would imply. One of them lies in the possibility that whoever proposes new policies may bring forward proposals which immediately put some participants at a dreadful tactical disadvantage. To avoid those proposals becoming government policy, the participants threatened by them might be willing to give up almost anything. Insistence upon the government's having to meet tests of rights and welfare would, it is true, mitigate this difficulty; but I cannot think of any certain formula for preventing some gains won in the bargaining process from consisting mainly in escaping from maliciously or gratuitously invented threats to the bargainers' interests.

On another approach to making evidence of bargaining evidence of benefits from bargaining, one might turn to stipulations about the initial resources of the participants or the kinds of bargains entered into. One might simply stipulate that the eligible participants all have equal resources, in money, in other material things, in trained and natural capacities, and in tactical position. This stipulation has the attraction of bypassing all the defects of democratic practice that notoriously arise from inequality of resources; but it has overwhelming drawbacks. It is hard to imagine how equality in tactical position could be achieved even in a direct democracy and leave (say) government officials with their special roles and authority. It violently contravenes the most familiar facts to suppose that without careful selection any numerous set of men would all turn out to have equal skill in bargaining. Inequality in material resources is also a familiar fact, which has been modified, but not eliminated, even in those societies that have abolished private property in the means of production.

Can a government meet a democratic test respecting collective preference when inequality exists in material resources and other resources as well? Perhaps if certain kinds of bargains were excluded, it could be held to meet such a test in meeting the bargaining test. One would want to exclude bargains between citizens and officials in which money was exchanged for favorable decisions on policies. I believe that advocates of democracy would also want to exclude bargains in which money was exchanged for votes, though there may be circumstances in which poor voters could gain more by this practice than otherwise.

The permissible kinds of bargains, those remaining, would include such things as trading votes on policies voted upon in order to reach agreements about policies not voted upon; and pledging mutual support, including supplies of funds, for common enterprises. Thus citizens would agree to cooperate fully with officials —even to the extent of contributing private funds— if the policies at issue in the bargaining were amended in certain ways. Or they would agree among themselves, in response to suggestions by their representatives or officials, to accept a proposal without voting, on condition that one lot vote for another policy that a second lot dearly wanted, and the second lot vice versa.

I conjecture that the existence of inequalities in the resources held by citizens does not by itself disqualify a government from being acceptable to advocates of democracy. Governments in the real world, such as the government of Switzerland, are generally accounted democratic in spite of inequalities in the resources of their citizens. In a New England town meeting, men with $1,000 a year come together with men 100 times richer; yet a New England town meeting exemplifies direct democracy. If a government passed the mandate test considered earlier, it would meet democratic demands regarding collective preference in spite of inequalities among the voters, though it might not even so be a good government in the eyes of democrats, if it failed the rights test or the welfare test.

Does the room that the present test gives for arriving at government policy through bargaining change the impact of unequal resources and make their existence a disqualification? Such inequality may be objectionable in itself; some advocates of democracy may find it distasteful that some citizens should have 100 times as much income as some others, even though these others perhaps enjoy a reasonable standard of living. Or inequality may leave some people in misery while others live in luxury; then it is objectionable, not merely in itself, but because of associations adverse to human welfare. Both these considerations, however, seem independent of questions of collective preference and bargaining. There must be many advocates of democracy, certainly in the United States, who do not object to inequality (of resources) in itself. They can hold this position without taking any position on bargaining. Inequality with adverse associations respecting welfare would call for application of welfare tests; but this application would not imply that the inequality thus condemned resulted from bargaining or was thereby aggravated; further reasoning would be required to show that.

The trouble with inequality of resources, in connection with bargaining, lies in the probability that those with larger resources will have advantages in bargaining over other participants. The extent of these advantages, however, is indeterminate. One important kind of advantage often associated with inequality of resources lies in the capacity of private employers to intimidate their employees. This kind of advantage, however, is something that we may rule out in setting up the bargaining test, as in setting up the others. We presume that in their political activities participants are free from intimidation—a freedom that might be guaranteed by a right to a livelihood and by such devices as the secret ballot.

Another kind of advantage lies in the fact that some of the things that the poor wanted—whether these are to be government policies or private undertakings—might depend more on the cooperation of the rich, with the large resources at their disposal, than on the cooperation of other people. But just what this kind of advantage amounted to and how it affected bargaining would vary with circumstances.

So would a third kind of advantage, the capacity of the rich to pursue more elaborate strategies in bargaining than the poor, who may not be able to hedge their bets. This advantage might be offset to a degree by some of the rich having inherited their resources without inheriting the bargaining skill of the men who built the resources up; and by the poor standing to gain subjectively more from bargaining than the rich, who give up resources less valuable to them because there are plenty more left.

I conclude that the charges that inequality of resources will adversely affect bargaining are sufficiently indeterminate *a priori* not to destroy the attractions of the bargaining test. I do not deny that inequality presents real dangers; but there are defenses against these dangers in the rights and welfare tests. There is also the defense built into the present test, of the poor being able to take recourse, if bargaining goes against them, by calling for a vote. We have already stipulated that this recourse is to be available on reasonably easy terms.

2 / An Indirect Test

2.1. Need for an Indirect Test

Neither of the direct tests I have examined embraces all the characteristics of performance that advocates of democracy might wish to find in a government. Other tests—concerned for example with rights and concerned with welfare—must be called in to supplement any test of collective preference. But the two direct tests do not even cover collective preference in a thoroughly desirable way. Both have acquired features by stipulation; and those features are to some degree arbitrary in formulation; they may have been set arbitrarily too low (or too high). The tests are, furthermore, both imperfect in their provisions for expressing intensities of preference. One test does not take voters' 2nd, 3rd, . . . and nth preferences into account at all, much less the varying intensities of hope or fear that accompany such preferences. The other test, in the room that it opens for bargaining, makes some provision for voters to trade away policies that they care little about in order (say) to forestall policies that frighten them. The provision, however, is very imperfect, and susceptible, with various distributions of bargaining advantages, to grave abuses.

I contend that these and other imperfections are things that advocates of democracy will put up with. Our object, after all, has not been to find tests that would lay to rest all misgivings, but just tests that will pass muster. Each of them is to give substantial satisfaction to democratic demands respecting the expression of collective preference, though none of them is to pretend to be the only means of satisfying those demands. Now the majority mandate test, incorporating as it does a paradigm of democratic choice, seems to be satisfactory pretty well beyond question. With somewhat less confidence, I hold that the bargaining test preserves enough of the spirit and features of the majority mandate test to be satisfactory, too. Paradoxically, it is by weakening the bargaining test (in its strongest part) that I now propose to go forward from the direct tests to discover an indirect test applicable to complex modern representative governments.

An indirect test, which would apply to representative governments only, is desirable because every important modern government with a claim to being democratic relies so much on representation as to practically ensure its failing any of the direct tests.

The failure, I have suggested, may not be entirely inevitable. One can imagine Iceland, or perhaps even Denmark, arranging for referendums in sufficient quantity and variety to pass the mandate test or at least the bargaining test (though these arrangements do not in fact exist). There is perhaps even some very slim chance that some government passes the bargaining test under its present arrangements. If choices of candidates for government office are counted as policy choices—choices of such policies as, for example, the policy that C rather than D shall be in a given office for a stated term—perhaps some government now holds sufficiently numerous countrywide elections to have the stipulated minimum number of policies adopted by voting. (One election might be enough, if 50 officials were elected from the country as a whole not as one slate, but each for himself.) However, I do not know of such a government; and I think none of the governments that I do know of—not even Iceland or Denmark—are going to modify their arrangements so as to have a chance of passing one of the direct tests.

From the fact that many, perhaps most, advocates of democracy believe themselves to be living under democratic government, one may reasonably infer that the tests which they would impose on governments are tests which some existing governments could pass, including their own. Aware in varying degrees of the imperfections of American government, most advocates of democracy would consider that the United States is somehow a democracy. The fact that it obviously is not a direct democracy evidently does not prevent this belief from developing.

The belief would be vindicated if a test satisfactory to advocates of democracy can be constructed which a complex representative government like that of the United States would pass. Now, retaining as much in the way of persuasive connections with the direct tests as possible would help make such an indirect test satisfactory; for the direct tests are based on a paradigm of democratic expression of collective preference. So I shall now try to construct an indirect test, which departs from the direct tests as little as possible, yet departs far enough to be capable of dealing with American government, which I assume to be, among putatively democratic governments, an extreme case of indirectness and complexity. The departures will inevitably be very considerable; we cannot therefore assume at the outset that the inquiry will lead to success. Possibly no indirect test can be found that retains persuasive connections with the direct tests and still accommodates American government. This negative finding, once it were obtained and reflected upon, might lead advocates of democracy to revise their beliefs and conclude that whatever its merits otherwise the government of the United States was not even in a loose sense a democracy. But let us not foreclose the issue without making the attempt at construction.

As an aid to construction, I shall first propound a contemporary rationale of American government, from which guidelines as to suitable modifications of the direct tests will emerge. (I say "contemporary," though the rationale did not anticipate recent catastrophes of foreign and domestic policy, and hence may already be less persuasive than it was only a few years ago; it remains the most recent of comprehensive and firmly articulated rationales.) After propounding the rationale, I shall proceed to the construction proper, which may be carried out fairly quickly, given the capital equipment that we shall have built up by that time in the argument of the previous sections and the section now immediately forthcoming. Finally, I shall consider how far the constructed test consists merely in palliating defects of the means that American government supplies for expressing collective preference; and thus constitutes no true test at all.

2.2. A Contemporary Rationale of American Government

The political system of the United States, considering both its constitutional arrangements and the activities of political parties and interest groups, may be looked upon as consisting of a complex of different forms for expressing collective preference. These forms offer so many different opportunities for majorities to determine policies, or at any rate to take recourse against policies determined otherwise.

Majorities formed in a number of different, sometimes overlapping constituencies determine the special cases of policies as to which candidates shall occupy given offices for forthcoming terms. Thus majorities —usually, though not always, both majorities in a sufficient number of states to control the Electoral College and a majority of the voters in the country— determine who will be President; majorities in the several states determine who will be United States Senators; majorities in the several constituencies, who will be Congressmen. (I disregard, in all cases, the complication that sometimes, because of the presence of third and fourth candidates, etc., a candidate will win without a majority, having only a plurality. The rationale tolerates the complication as exceptional.) Majorities also elect the governors and legislators of the states; and the representatives, executive and legislative, who function in myriad localities within the states—towns and school regions and sewer districts.

Does majority determination of the policies about who shall hold office carry over to determining the other policies of American government? There are two main kinds of relations to be considered in this connection: what I shall call "first tier" relations, which hold (or fail to hold) between the voters in a given constituency and undertakings by the candidate (or candidates) elected therein; and also what I shall call "second tier" relations, which hold between the voters in the country as a whole and the policies arrived at by their representatives.

Suppose that a candidate, undertaking to support a number of policies P, Q, R, etc., wins a majority of votes in a given constituency, simultaneously defeating an opposing candidate who has denounced at least one of these policies. I assume further that the voters have made or could produce weak orderings for each of these policies and for the alternatives to it (e.g., for P_1 versus P_2 or P_3 or P_4 etc.; and for Q_1 versus Q_2 or Q_3 or Q_4 etc.); that they have (in sufficient proportion) found genuine alternatives of policy in the differences between the undertakings of the winning candidate and those of the losing one; and that they have voted accordingly.

Then the following possibilities exist as regards the significance of the majority vote for the winning candidate:

In all cases, the majority will have been composed of voters each of whom has ranked the combination of policies supported by the winning candidate above the combination of policies supported by the losing one. (However, consistently with doing so when comparing the combinations, any given voter belonging to the majority may have given some first-place rankings to policies supported by the losing candidate alone; and possibly have given no first-place rankings to any policy supported by the winning candidate. The winning candidate may have won his vote by offering more second- and third-place policies.)

(1) There may in some cases be a majority (identical with the winning majority or a subset of that majority) consisting of voters all of whom rank each of the policies supported by the winning candidate ahead of all the alternatives to it, including the alternative offered by the losing candidate where this is different.

(2) (a) There may be a majority (identical with the winning majority or a subset) each of whom ranks all of the policies in some subset of the policies supported by the winning candidate ahead respectively of the alternatives to them. (b) Furthermore, the remaining policies among those supported by the winning candidate may each be ranked ahead of all the alternatives to them by some voters (who may or may

not have voted in the end with the winning majority). When all the voters with these first-place rankings are added up, they may form a majority of minorities for the combination of remaining policies.

(3) There may be a majority who have voted for the winning candidate as in (2)(a) without there being a majority of minorities for the remaining combination of his policies as in (2)(b).

(4) There may be no majority of voters who give first-place ranking to any of the policies supported by the winning candidate; but there may be a majority of minorities who give first-place rankings to policies in some subset of the policies supported by him, and who have formed the winning majority or a subset of it.

(5) There may be no majority identical with the winning majority or a subset of it who give first-place ranking to any of the policies supported by the winning candidate x and there may be no majority of minorities who have voted for him because of their first-place rankings of policies in some subset of those supported by him. His majority may have depended on the preference of some of the voters for the combination of second-place, third-place, and lower-place policies offered by him, as against the combination of (say) fewer second- and third-place and more lower-place policies offered by his opponent. I shall call such a majority a "second-choice majority."

Of these possibilities, only the first connects collective preference with each of the policies at issue in the way that advocates of democracy would ideally want; but there may be substantial satisfaction for their demands in the second, third, and fourth cases. Even the fifth possibility, which is consistent with there being no one (apart from the candidate himself) who ranks any of the policies supported by the winning candidate ahead of the alternatives to it, is something that advocates of democracy may reconcile themselves to. In itself, a second-choice majority establishes a significant positive first tier relation between collective preference and policies. Moreover, there are processes at work tending to convert cases like the fifth one into one of the other cases—at least into (2), (3), or (4) (which I shall not attempt to rank among themselves). On every issue, a first-place majority is liable to be formed. Candidates will not let such a majority be formed against one of their undertakings if they can help it; and they have a powerful, though not conclusive, incentive to offer in respect to any given issue an undertaking that will attract a majority of first-place rankings.

The possibility of an unfavorable majority being formed on any issue, coupled with the further possibility that disfavor on this issue may lead to an unfavorable vote at election time, operates as a limit on the adoption of policies that do not have majorities behind them. This limit, conforming to the desires of democrats, protects majorities from being actually oppressed and victimized by minority policies. Furthermore, a second-choice majority operates closer to the limit than the majorities available in the other cases. Other things being equal, it may be held, a prudent politician will try to elicit the stronger support, more satisfactory to advocates of democracy, that musters behind policies in the other cases. He will shape his commitments to policy accordingly.

In general, the necessity of winning a majority of votes compels candidates to undertake no policy that threatens a majority too drastically, for the system provides any majority in the constituency with a means of recourse against such threats. Moreover, the system encourages a candidate to support any policy that he believes a majority will support; to do otherwise, when he does not have to choose between conflicting policies, or give up a definite opportunity to assemble a majority of minorities, increases his risks gratuitously.

Hence it appears that in the sort of first tier relations characteristic of American constituencies majorities do influence in an important way—loosely, but not ineffectively—what policies winning candidates undertake to support while in office. If the winning candidates cannot escape from their undertakings, and they occupy offices in which they themselves promulgate policies for their constituencies, then majorities in the constituencies will have influenced—in the same loose but effective way—the policies actually followed by the government.

In second tier relations of the sort existing in American government, determination of policy becomes complicated by the necessity for representatives from the several constituencies to come together and jointly settle upon the policies which the government will actually follow. In becoming more complicated, however, determination does not necessarily accord majorities less influence. Indeed, confrontation with other representatives further helps check the representative of any one constituency from flouting majority preferences in his community too violently; for his constituents will be likely to have allies in other constituencies. Confrontation with representatives from overlapping constituencies (the House versus the Senate; or Congress versus the President) works much the same way, this time by bringing into play majorities differently formed to offset the contingent peculiarities of any one constituency and its representative. The checks also, of course, help to protect the *minorities* of any one constituency from being grossly victimized.

Himself backed in one or another of the listed first

tier senses by a majority of his constituents, a winning candidate taking office in the second tier confronts the representatives of other constituencies, each of them bearing majority endorsement in a first tier sense. (Again I disregard plurality victories as exceptional.) On every policy issue that these representatives now discuss together at least a majority of them will have to agree. Almost any given candidate will seek to be in the majority on some issues. To achieve victory on these issues he will seek to combine his votes with those of other representatives who have been elected with the same undertakings in regard to those issues. But these undertakings will sometimes, for example, have been backed by first-place majorities in different constituencies. Representatives who have obtained such backing and know it will have an important incentive to stand by it and bargain away less strongly backed undertakings instead if they must bargain away any. Hence there will be a powerful tendency for majorities in the constituencies to be reflected by majorities in the representative body.

One cannot quite guarantee the possibility of ordering the undertakings on any given issue so that they range from those expected to do most in some respect of policy to those expected to do least. But usually this possibility does exist. If it is not visible (say in different amounts of proposed expenditures) the representatives have an important incentive to find some feature or other of the undertakings that will realize such an ordering. (The issue may be reformulated in order to realize it.) Given such an ordering, it becomes clear how a compromise can be reached; and the compromise will be one satisfactory to a majority of representatives. It will have the form of doing just enough in the respect of policy on which the ordering is based to be compatible with the undertakings of a majority of the representatives; and these undertakings will be under the control, substantial though imperfect, of first tier majorities in the constituencies.

Thus, in second tier relations as well as in first tier ones, majorities in the constituencies strongly influence the policies actually followed by American government. Again, the influence falls short of being precise or conclusive. Because representatives differ in the intensities of preference that they and their constituents feel in respect to various issues, they may be impelled to trade away votes on some issues in order to gain support on others. In consequence, there is a possibility that many policies—perhaps all policies—emerging from the representative body have only the backing offered by a second-choice majority among the representatives—a second-choice majority in the second tier, itself possibly backed only by second-choice majorities in the constituencies of the first tier. Nevertheless, even results like these—taken together, the farthest departure possible from straightforward correspondence with majority preferences in the constituencies—will have conformed in some degree to the principle of majority rule. Departures that would arouse majority opposition in the constituencies will have been avoided; the representatives who finally settle upon a policy will have risked with each of their undertakings the chance that their rivals could mobilize a majority against them. Moreover, majority backing for any given policy will always be favored to some extent when it can be achieved. Tantalizingly inconclusive though its operation may be, the majority principle steadily operates as a force attracting final policies toward points on which majorities in the representative body converge with majorities in the constituencies.

An effective contemporary rationale of American government cannot, however, rest content with this plausible picture; for all its concessions, the picture remains idealized. Many facts about American politics, once they are brought into play, cast an unfavorable light on the workings of its electoral arrangements. For one thing, large proportions of those eligible to vote in American elections do not participate. For another, those who do participate do not most of them cast their votes in the light of specific policy undertakings by the candidates. (They vote instead out of party loyalty, or out of party loyalty reinforced by family traditions and religious affiliation.) Finally, American constituencies are notoriously so unequal in population that majorities in representative bodies may easily have obtained the backing of only a small minority of voters in the constituencies. Reapportionment, following recent decisions of the Supreme Court, has been reducing this particular drawback, but at best the reduction will go only part way; it will leave the constituencies of United States Senators unequal, for example, since every state is constitutionally entitled to two Senators regardless of population.

At this point, the contemporary rationale turns first to the two major political parties and second to the interest groups. The activities of the parties and of the interest groups, it may be held, complement each other; and offset the deficiencies just mentioned.

The parties, competing with one another for control of the government, dramatize elections, excite the electorate to some degree, and elicit broader participation than would occur otherwise. They assist in offering the voters some choice of policies. The Republican and Democratic parties, it is true, each embrace politicians of very diverse outlooks; the party platforms overlap on some issues, straddle others, and generally differ only incrementally on the issues that remain. Nevertheless, a vote cast for a Republican candidate, tending to put the Republican party in control, predictably favors some policies over others—policies less likely to interfere with business practices, for example; and policies tender toward the interests of large commercial farmers. Voting by family tradition and religious allegiance makes some sense when it is related to these broad differences between parties in overall orientation. Historically, the Democratic party has demonstrated more sympathy for the urban immigrant masses, largely Catholic; the Republican party, for independent farmers and businessmen in rural communities, mainly Protestant.

The activity of the parties not only produces a broad differentiation between the sets of candidates that they respectively offer. Their activity coordinates the positions on policy that elected candidates bring into legislative discussions. Since the coordination reflects in each party its overall orientation, the coordination helps ensure that the candidates once elected will by and large operate in ways that the voters may predict. Finally, by campaigning across the country, the parties to some extent coordinate the undertakings made by its candidates in different constituencies. Thus they reduce the chances of concentrated minorities (or, indeed, of concentrated majorities) controlling the government; for the probability of this happening (which may be aggravated by constituencies being unequal in population, but does not depend on their being so) diminishes as each party gathers countrywide support.

No one would pretend that the activity of the major American parties fully succeeds in doing any of these helpful things; but that is no reason for despising what the parties in fact do. Moreover, just as they help to repair the deficiencies of the formal arrangements for voting and representation, so, it may be argued, their own deficiencies, and the formal deficiencies so far as they do not remedy them, are in a substantial way repaired by the activity of interest groups.

The complex of interest groups—commercial, vocational, religious, charitable, idealistic—express the variously assorted preferences of the people and arrange for these preferences to be reflected in policy according both to the numbers sharing them and the intensity with which they are felt. Because the interest groups are specialized in their concern with issues, they can evaluate the impact of policies in more detail than parties can. They know more about the preferences of the people that they represent and more about the features of policy required to meet those preferences. Furthermore, their very existence normally signalizes in each case a serious and permanent concern with policies of certain sorts—concern that may well deserve more attention, even if only a minority of the population in each case has it to a pronounced degree, than casual and transitory opinions afloat at election times. Detailed determination of the policies actually followed by the government may, therefore, be assigned to the bargaining carried on by interest groups with representatives and other government officials (and also with the party organizations). Ideally, one might hope that the interest groups would in effect adjust the combination of policies followed by the government to at least the support of a countrywide majority of minorities, the minorities in each case obtaining something they intensely prefer.

Might not certain interest groups enjoy undue advantages, however, from having greater funds, more expert lobbyists, perhaps fewer scruples, or simply a more alert membership? Even more disturbing to contemplate, one might cite the dangers posed for inarticulate and unorganized segments of the population.

The rationale offers several answers to these objections. It points out that interest groups are subject to a variety of internal restraints. The members of any given interest group vary in commitment and activity, not only for reasons of temperament and character, but also because they may belong to other groups as well, which perhaps pursue interests in conflict with those championed by the present group. If the leaders of the groups take extreme positions, they risk alienating considerable proportions of their own overlapping memberships. The rationale mentions, further, the opportunity that exists for organizing new groups, which are liable to spring up when government policy becomes palpably adverse to any part of the population. It speaks hopefully of the attention that the permanent administrative officials of the government may give inarticulate and unorganized groups.

The rationale (as I shall formulate it here) relies mainly, however, upon the major parties to act so as to forestall outrages upon particular groups, and especially outrages that offend majority sentiment. According to the rationale, the major American parties provide an institutional framework—besides the inadequate one provided by the formal constitutional arrangements—within which the interest groups are forced to bargain with one another. Interest groups that refuse to bargain, or which attempt outrages, offer tempting targets which neither party can safely stand near and which both have powerful incentives to attack. But interest groups, in their turn, must fear being isolated in this way; to forestall being isolated, they seek influence in both parties and to gain it agree to bargains with the other groups forming each party's clientele. Because the clienteles of the two parties so largely overlap, the differences between the parties remain moderate; competition between them does not become pathologically destructive. It is safe for the parties to compete on issues so long as the parties have to reconcile the demands of broad and overlapping assortments of interest groups—assortments embracing majorities of the population on each side. On the other hand it is safe—indeed, useful—for interest groups to determine the details of policies so long as the framework provided by competitive major parties forces the groups concerned with every given issue to bargain with one another.

2.3. Extracting a Test from the Rationale

I believe that advocates of democracy would find the rationale just outlined at least arresting, and persuasive waiving certain troublesome points. Many advocates of democracy have in fact found it persuasive as it stands. But so far as it is persuasive, the rationale may be conjectured to imply that something like a satisfactory indirect test for democratic performance respecting the expression of collective preference has been passed. I shall now do something to vindicate this conjecture by extracting such a test from the rationale, simultaneously arranging to take care of some of the points that the rationale leaves troublingly unsettled.

The test that I extract calls for two calculations: first, calculation of the results as to the policies that would have been adopted by the government if glaring deficiencies of present practice had been corrected in certain stipulated ways for the test period; second, calculation of how far the actual results, with those deficiencies operating, coincide with the results reached by the first calculation. In expounding the rationale, I deliberately left undetermined whether the rationale

209 / An Indirect Test

applied to the whole complex of American government or to the federal government; I shall work out
the present test for the federal government only.

First Calculation: Results with Deficiencies Corrected.
Let us assume the present formal arrangements for
electing representatives and officials of the federal government of the United States, the present major parties,
the present complex of interest groups, the present
procedures within the government itself for adopting
policies, and the present opportunities for bargaining.
Let us imagine, however, that the operation of the
electoral process has been corrected in certain ways.

We imagine, to begin with, that the participation
condition as stipulated for the mandate test is fulfilled
for the election of candidates in all constituencies. (At
present some constituencies, particularly those in the
South, fall far short of fulfillment.)

Consider next the two countrywide sets of constituencies relevant to federal elections: for Senators and
members of the Electoral College, the states; for Congressmen, the various districts. (To simplify matters,
I shall ignore Congressmen-at-large.) We imagine that
the constituencies in each of these sets has been equal-
ized in number of people eligible to vote, according
to the following plan, the use of which for one set
of constituencies shall not prejudice its imaginary use
for the other set: In constituencies now average or less
than average in number of people eligible to vote, the
present population remains there; from the constituencies larger than average in number of people eligible
to vote, randomly selected proportions of these people
are drawn and redistributed again at random to the
constituencies first mentioned, so as to make every
constituency equal by having the average number of
people eligible to vote. This imaginary operation, of

course, does some violence to the federal principle (violence mitigated by the extent to which the present population remains in place), but we are not now concerned to evaluate the merits of the United States as a federation, or even as a federation of democracies. We are concerned to discover whether the federal government is itself an acceptable sort of democracy.

The people who have actually run for office in the various constituencies during the test period we shall suppose were set aside when the random selections for redistributing people eligible to vote were drawn. Let us imagine that in these changed circumstances the candidates would run with the same frequency and against the same opposition in the general elections as they in fact do in uncorrected conditions. Now, as an approximation to meeting the condition of genuine alternatives, we suppose that the Republican and Democratic candidates in each constituency differentiate their undertakings with respect to at least one issue discussed before each election; that this issue is the one, of all those on which differentiation occurs in *any* constituency, that a majority of the people eligible to vote in this constituency (after redistribution) feel most intensely about (if such an issue exists); that in any case the undertakings appear sufficiently differentiated for a majority to weakly order one ahead of another; and that the differentiation be adequately publicized within the constituency, up to a standard of adequacy like that required by the bargaining test in connection with opportunities for bargaining. If in any constituency the Republican or Democratic candidate in fact runs unopposed in the general election by a candidate of the other major party, we imagine that a candidate of that party, meeting the condition about differentiation just stated but otherwise uncharacterized, appears to fill the gap. (I disregard, again, the possibility of third and fourth etc. candidates.)

The reassortment condition we shall leave aside until the second stage of the present test. We shall, however, do something at this stage about the sweep-through condition. Inspired by the measures taken in the bargaining test to approximate fulfilling this condition, we imagine that in every constituency some minimum number of the people eligible to vote (say 1 per cent) can through petition compel either candidate to state an undertaking with respect to any specific issue. This provision does not make the provisions for differentiation superfluous, since both candidates may adopt the same position on any issue brought into question by petition.

With the deficiencies of American political practice corrected as we have imagined, let the results of the elections held during the test period (which might be twelve years still) be calculated; and the results as to policy of elections and bargaining combined. The calculation shall make use of some serviceably complete description of the policies actually followed by the government, and report the results accordingly.

I quite realize that this demand, with which the tasks of the first stage of calculation come to an end, is so staggering that it may appear absurd. Political science, in its present state, is hardly prepared to meet the demand. But I do not suppose that the demand could be met quickly. Years of hard work by a great many dedicated political scientists would be needed to carry out a calculation of the sort envisaged; though once it had been carried out for the first time, it would be very much easier to do the job again. To do it the first time, more scientific theory would have to be built up identifying the factors that determine people to vote one way or another (when they vote at all). More theory would be needed locating the forces that act upon politicians and interest-group leaders engaged in bargaining. A great deal of information would have to be collected through public opinion surveys—some of it to further the construction of needed theory, some of it as an inevitable incident of calculation. (For example, sample surveys would be used to discover evidence bearing upon the effective realization of the petitioning provision.) Even with a great deal more theory and a great deal more information, the calculation will furnish only inexact results for many issues: broad limits within which the policies adopted would fall, rather than anything like logically equivalent formulations of their contents.

Even in its present state, however, political science could make some headway with the calculation demanded. The results of elections can be predicted with fair success on the basis of broad demographic characteristics, which could (I believe) be identified without too much trouble during the operation of imaginary redistribution. The demographic composition of the constituencies after redistribution would be known and its effect on elections in the constituencies would be predictable. Moreover, techniques like simulation with the use of high-speed computers can dramatically abridge the work of producing the predictions; and these techniques can be extended to cover the bargaining process and deliberations in the representative bodies.

The calculation called for in the first stage of the present test can therefore be considered feasible, though very laborious. (Yet the labor might be very worthwhile, among other reasons for the growth that it would foster in scientific political theory.)

Second Calculation: Matching Results. The calculation envisaged in the second stage of the present test consists simply in determining how far the actual policies followed by the federal government during the test period coincide with the policies arrived at by the calculation of the first stage. The special cases of policies that concern which candidates shall occupy which elective offices may be put aside, since the main interest of this test (like the earlier, direct ones) is to see whether collective preference is acceptably reflected in the other policies followed. To assure exact comparability between the actual results and the hypothetically calculated ones, the same (matching) serviceably complete description of policies will have to be used.

To make the test definite, I stipulate that in the case of at least two-thirds of the policies mentioned in the serviceably complete description the actual results shall coincide with the hypothetically calculated ones; only then is the government under test to be accepted as democratically heeding collective preference.

The test will gain an important attraction if something approximating the reassortment condition can be attached to it. There are difficulties about doing so. The number of elections in which any given voter can participate may not suffice to give room for reassortment to operate, and would fail to relate reassortment to policies other than choices of candidates anyway. One might survey through samples the preferences that people eligible to vote would express for various policies if they were given chances to vote directly on them. But since most voters inevitably know nothing significant about most policies followed by the United States federal government, one could not hope for significant information from every voter over the whole range of policies. Consequently, the reassortment condition as modified for the present test would not aim so high. It might take the following form: No voter shall be in the minority on more than 90 per cent of those issues discussed during the test period with which he is acquainted (in some testably minimum degree); and each of 90 per cent of the voters shall be in the majority on at least one-third of such issues.

On the present test, then, the government will be accepted as democratic in respect to collective preference if and only if there is at least two-thirds coincidence in the matching described and the modified reassortment condition is fulfilled.

The provision for matching offers a way of answering one major doubt about the contemporary rationale of American government. The rationale suggests parties and interest groups act in various ways to compensate for some of the defects in the formal arrangements of the system. The suggestion compels respect—but respect does not prevent the question arising, just how effective are the compensations? The provision for matching helps determine how effective. Moreover, our imaginary operations have set the standard against which matching is to take place—the results as calculated in the first stage of the test—reasonably high, in respect to just those defects of the formal arrangements that seemed most troublesome.

Advocates of democracy may be persuaded to accept the present test, *faute de mieux,* by conceiving of it as an indirect substitute for the direct bargaining test. That test relied in large part on bargaining possibly as selective in participants and as comprehensive in topics as the bargaining envisaged in the present test. It did, as the present test does not, call for a number of direct votes upon policies other than the election of candidates for office; and it provided for easy recourse to such votes, while the present test does not provide for recourse to them at all. Yet the recourse actually envisaged by the present test, of being able to shift votes between candidates of competing parties, and moreover bring influence to bear through the activity of interest groups, seems far from negligible; and by the provisions for differentiation and petitioning the test applies a hypothetical standard more exacting than the actual arrangements. Majority rule does operate through these provisions, and one may consider that an indirect test cannot demand its operating any more fully. Binding elected representatives so closely as to forestall bargaining without producing deadlock in the second tier, would, for example, require the voters in each constituency to have more information about all policies, including information about how other voters in other constituencies will be affected, than they could ever possibly have.

Yet some points of uneasiness remain, which apply to the rationale and which the extracted test has not disposed of. Voting for a candidate who may offer undertakings on a number of issues simultaneously offers only a very crude way for collective preference to come to bear on any one issue. On any single issue, even a majority cannot count on being decisive unless they are willing to concentrate on that issue alone. But how many issues ever become so salient? Interest groups have plenty of room to operate in dubious ways short of outrages that would make their conduct a salient issue, short even of creating unduly unfavorable publicity for themselves by offering momentary targets for politicians and other interest groups. Does not the present test very likely concede interest groups too much room for abuses of collective preference?

Unfortunately, it is in the present state of knowledge impossible to tell. Political science possesses neither sufficient formal theory about the operations of elections, bargaining, and policy determination nor sufficient suitably organized empirical information to describe exactly what happens to the whole range of issues treated as they pass through the federal system. There is in fact more formal theory on hand than I have made use of. There is also a great deal of information waiting to be systematically organized in ways corresponding to formal theory. Moreover, one may hope (given a reasonable amount of intelligent effort on the part of political scientists) for dramatic increases of knowledge in both respects. Present hopes do not amount to present knowledge, however. We do not now have enough systematic knowledge of the influence exerted by interest groups, for example, to be able to stipulate exactly what limitations we would wish to impose upon their activities.

Because the points of uneasiness that remain cannot be safely forgotten, I put forward the two-stage indirect test as a test to be accepted only for the time being, pending further efforts toward systematic political science.

2.4. Relevance and Efficacy of the Test

The present test, in which the effort to relate majority rule to the choice of policies in a complex representative government has tentatively culminated, anticipates certain features of the United States federal government. Does it perhaps suit the peculiar features of that government all too well, so that any answer that the test returned would come as a rationalization? The test may seem to pool the dubious features with the speciously good ones, so that the latter cover up the faults of the former in the overall picture at which the test aims.

I think that the test, as I have put it forward, quite

conclusively escapes the charge of rationalization. Even if the United States passed the test with flying colors, it would not necessarily gain the applause of democrats; for its policies might violate personal rights or neglect human welfare. In fact, I think, some policies of the federal government are bad ones in both these respects; but it is entirely possible that their badness originates not in defective provisions for the expression of collective preference, but in indifference, callousness, and stupidity on the part of American voters.

One might point out, further, that the basic idea of the test—of calculating in one stage what the results in policy would be if the constituencies were transformed in certain ways, then matching these results against the actual ones—does not presuppose there being anything especially desirable about the peculiar features of the United States government. The test could readily be modified to apply to other representative governments. Indeed, it would apply with less trouble to less complex systems like that of the Canadian federal government and the government of the United Kingdom. In both Canada and Britain, the imaginary operations called for would be less extensive. The constituencies, for example, are already less variable in population. In Britain, strict party discipline (some would say, overstrict) prevails during legislation. These and other features of government probably make it easier to calculate the hypothetical results that the present test would call for, modified to apply to Canada and Britain. The test could be modified in the opposite direction, to apply to some systems in which competition between candidates occurs not between parties, but within one party—as in Louisiana; or lately, in Tanzania.

The fact that I have put the test forward as a tentative measure opens up another route of escape from the charge of rationalization. The test is tentative because it is suggested that with further developments in political science a more exacting test—perhaps a series of progressively more exacting tests—can be found to replace it. Rationalizations are not usually accompanied by notices warning, "Doubtful on certain points; good for the time being only."

But perhaps they might be; perhaps the notion of a self-confessedly temporary rationalization makes sense, regardless of its unexpectedness. Perhaps, too, the fact that a government might fail other tests, having to do with rights and welfare, even if it passed this one, does not sufficiently mitigate the charge against this one.

My main answer to the charge of rationalization relies on this fact about the present test: No one knows whether the United States federal government does actually pass it. As I have remarked before, years of work would be required to find out. The work would inevitably extend systematic political science to the point at which a stricter test could be substituted. But even the results on the present test would be worth having. They would indicate whether or not a certain limited kind of correspondence between the preferences of the voters and the policies of the government obtains. The fact that the government might turn out to fail the test indicates that the test has one of the chief features of a genuine test. The feature suffices, I think, to save it from the charge of rationalization.

The fact that the federal government might fail the test does, however, expose the test to something like ridicule from the opposite point of view. Is there not something far-fetched about elaborating a test that calls for so much protracted research? I have supposed from the beginning that advocates of democracy think of themselves as living in democracies, if they live in countries like the United States. Surely they would say that the United States is a democracy, without requiring protracted research of themselves; and I have argued all along that their saying a government is democratic implies its policies have a certain relation to the collective preference of its citizens. What this relation comprises can in part be gathered from what else advocates of democracy say and in part be extracted by dialectic.

I accept all these points; yet I think a test that the United States might fail can be consistently extracted. Whether the federal government of the United States democratically reflects collective preference in the policies it pursues is not, I think, a question that can be answered offhand (unless we apply a direct test, which any tolerably complex representative government will surely fail). It is, compared to questions about rights or welfare, something hard to determine, partly from want of evidence, partly from uncertainty in our usage and partly because the question is meant to be left open.

When advocates of democracy call the United States a democracy, I think they do so on the one hand relying on cruder tests than I have considered—for example, simply on the evidence that most adults are eligible to vote and vote if they care to without intimidation; and on the other hand hoping that they are right. They hope, first, that the evidence will bear them out by vindicating the suggestions of the contemporary rationale in some such way as the indirect test here offered might vindicate the suggestions. They hope, second, that the United States will improve in performance, so that in time it will pass successively stricter tests as to collective preference (and other matters). It is on this hope that I found my contention that the question whether the United States is democratically governed is meant to be left open. Democracy, as advocates of democracy understand it, is an ideal that may be expected to become more exacting with time and practice. The present test falls short in some respects of the present ideal; it perhaps shoots ahead of present practice; maybe it runs just abreast of the present limits of practical reform.

EPILOGUE

The character of my argument with respect to personal rights and human welfare has differed asymmetrically from the character of my argument with respect to collective preference. I have spent a lot of time explaining what the concepts of rights and welfare meant; and very little time formulating the tests that I anticipate advocates of democracy using on these topics. By contrast, I have spent just about the whole of the time and space devoted to collective preference formulating, or trying to formulate, a usable test; I explained what collective preference meant only in the course of working out the test.

This asymmetry of treatment may be justified, I think, by the present condition of the concepts examined. The root ideas involved in the concept of rights and the concept of welfare either require some digging to expose or need to be freed from the debris of philosophical controversy. By contrast, the root idea involved in the democratic concept of collective preference—which I have taken to be majority rule, in the direct mandate sense—seems quite obvious. Yet just how it is to be used to evaluate a complex representative government seems very difficult to make out; whereas once the concepts of rights and of welfare have been clarified, there is no difficulty in seeing what simple and relevant tests they engender.

A further asymmetry has emerged in my results. The United States and Canada and many other countries professing to have democratic governments pretty clearly would fail the tests I have formulated respecting rights and welfare. How they would fare on the test of collective preference, on the other hand, no one could easily predict.

I think circumstances justify this asymmetry, too. Surely most people are aware how imperfect the performance of the United States and Canada is respecting rights and welfare. A test of rights or welfare that did not reflect these imperfections would carry no conviction. On the other hand, many people are inclined to think that the United States and Canada and a number of other countries would pass some reasonable democratic test respecting collective preference. At any rate, they would think a test unreasonable that those countries were bound to fail just because they inevitably had complex representative governments.

The tests would no doubt create a very different impression if they were used not absolutely, as minimum standards to be passed by each government pretending to be acceptable, taken by itself, to advocates of democracy; but rather as a basis for comparing governments admittedly liable to be grossly imperfect in all three respects. I have concentrated on formulating the tests as absolute ones; but I by no means reject the possibility of using them as the basis for comparative tests. On the contrary, I have sought to formulate absolute tests that would establish a reasonable basis for comparative tests, which in the real world are unavoidable, significant, and morally compelling.

The United States and Canada would look much better—and properly so—on comparative tests of performance.

All governments are imperfect; and all would-be democratic governments are imperfectly democratic. Yet, compared to other imperfect governments falling outside a select circle in which the United States would be grouped with Canada, countries in northwestern Europe, and a few countries elsewhere, the United States, for instance, may well be obviously better in its performance respecting collective preference.

Conclusive comparisons favoring the United States in respect to rights or welfare might not be so numerous. Clearly it does better than the Communist countries as regards civil liberties and associated aspects of personal freedom; as well or better as regards the right to a livelihood; perhaps not so well as regards the right to civic benefits, or the right to political participation. As regards welfare, when adjustments have been made for differences in *per capita* wealth, the United States might lose any conclusive advantage over, say, Poland or Cuba or the Soviet Union. It would still (perhaps together with the governments of those countries) belong to a class of governments each of which performed better on the human welfare test than any of the numerous governments probably not included in the class.

The fact that the United States would probably turn out ahead respecting collective preference without being behind respecting rights or welfare means that the three tests taken together favor the United States. Yet they do not give Americans any grounds for complacency. It is shameful that a government so rich in resources should do less than the best done anywhere in the world in any category of welfare; shameful, too, that a government so committed by tradition to rights should have been so backward in enforcing some or even in recognizing others.

Let us be very clear also that a government may do very well, comparatively or even absolutely, on all three tests formulated in this book; and yet pursue wicked policies. The tests all concern domestic performance or domestic approval of performance wherever it occurs. Now, a government may be very acceptably democratic by domestic tests, and do great good for most of its own people. Yet abroad it may pursue belligerent policies, callously devastating other countries, and cruelly subordinating the interests of their peoples to the supposed interests of its own. Being democratic, so far as it is democratic, will not excuse such a government, nor will its domestic benefits; being democratic will only spread the blame.

Bibliography

1) The concepts of equality, liberty, and justice, given only incidental treatment in this book, and that treatment often only implicit, have the next claim on the reader's attention. There are treatments available of these concepts that accomplish many or most of the things that I have aimed at doing in treating the concepts of rights, welfare, and collective preference. The existence of these treatments led me to concentrate upon trying to explicate the latter concepts. Whether or not my aims with these have been accomplished, I think that there is no other published work that does for them what has been done for equality, liberty, and justice, in showing what the concepts mean to ordinary advocates of democracy as instruments for evaluating governments and policies.

On equality, there is a near-contemporary classic to turn to, by an historian of great philosophical acuteness: R. H. Tawney's *Equality*, 4th ed. (London: George Allen & Unwin, 1952). One will soon also be able to consult, in the forthcoming *International Encyclopedia of the Social Sciences*, what promises to be an exceptionally instructive article on equality by Felix E. Oppenheim, which I have seen in draft form.

Another of Oppenheim's works seems to me to be the first thing to consult on the concept of liberty—at any rate, the first thing to consult after paying due and serious respect to John Stuart Mill's noble book *On Liberty* (London, 1859). In this case the work is Oppenheim's *Dimensions of Freedom* (New York: St. Martin's Press, 1961), which as my review of it in *The Philosophical Review*, LXXII (October 1963), 524–28, shows, I regard as needing important rectifications, but nonetheless as an invaluable contribution, the present point of departure for all serious further discussion.

On justice, the chief writings to recommend are articles by John Rawls, especially "Justice as Fairness," *The Philosophical Review*, LXVII (April 1958), 164–94, and "The Sense of Justice," *The Philosophical Review*, LXXII (July 1963), 281–305; and, when it comes out, his long-awaited book on the subject. Nicholas Rescher's recent book, *Distributive Justice* (Indianapolis: Bobbs-Merrill, 1966), illuminates many important features of the concept in the course of discussing the challenges that it poses for certain varieties of utilitarianism.

2) My general approach in this book, directed as it is toward formulating a series of tests for governments, owes something to T. D. Weldon's well-known—perhaps notorious—Pelican *The Vocabulary of Politics* (London: Penguin, 1953). Weldon's conception of linguistic analysis was simple, extreme, and superficial; and I think in his outburst he went much too far casting out the various traditional topics of political philosophy. Yet I think his book blew a lot of fresh cold air into the subject. I appreciate in particular his useful separation of questions about the intelligibility of tests from questions about moral foundations. Unlike him, I consider the separation advisable only for particular purposes; but such a particular purpose has brought me through the present book.

3) My treatment of the concept of rights was strongly influenced in its inception by A. I. Melden's *Rights and Right Conduct* (Oxford: Basil Blackwell, 1959). In its present form, it resembles the treatment given by Hans Kelsen, in his *General Theory of Law and State*, translated by Anders Wedberg (Cambridge: Harvard University Press, 1945), pp. 75–90, more than any other. Besides recommending these books, I would mention the treatment of rights in W. D. Lamont, *The Principles of*

Moral Judgement (Oxford: The Clarendon Press, 1946), pp. 70–78, and in H. L. A. Hart, "Are There Any Natural Rights?" *The Philosophical Review*, LXIV (April 1955), 175–91, both of which I have had in mind while writing myself, though I happen to disagree in important ways with Hart's argument. In my latest amendments to the part on rights, I have also been responding to what G. H. von Wright says in *Norm and Action* (London: Routledge & Kegan Paul, 1963) about rights and about a suggested distinction between norms and normative statements; I respond, but again I disagree.

For an extended discussion of the distinction between act-utilitarianism and rule-utilitarianism, the reader might do worse than consult my article, "The Choice Between Utilitarianisms," in the *American Philosophical Quarterly*, IV (January 1967), 28–38.

In *The Political Theory of Possessive Individualism* (Oxford: The Clarendon Press, 1962), C. B. MacPherson offers a much more intricate analysis of Locke's doctrine of private property than I attempt to give. I think, with some reservations, that his account is closer to Locke's intentions than mine; but I think mine—Locke simplified —may better represent how Locke was commonly understood, especially in America. I have found another useful aid to my reading of Locke in Robert A. Goldwin's essay in Leo Strauss and Joseph Cropsey, eds., *History of Political Philosophy* (Chicago: Rand McNally, 1963). Charles A. Reich's articles, "The New Property," *Yale Law Journal*, LXXIII (April 1964), 733–87, and "Individual Rights and Social Welfare: The Emerging Legal Issues," *Yale Law Journal*, LXXIV (June 1965), 1,245–57, make some interesting points, with arresting examples, about the need for recognizing new personal rights to prevent abuses of the comprehensive welfare policies that governments now undertake.

4) The current philosophical literature on welfare—

subtle in development, mistaken in point of departure—has been the work of economists rather than of philosophers. It originates in economists' dissatisfaction with Benthamite utilitarianism on the point of intelligibility. (Philosophers have been inclined to waive the question of intelligibility in their zeal to score moral points against utilitarianism in any form.)

Pareto led the economists' retreat from the hedonistic calculus; he defines his welfare criterion, stated for preferences rather than objectively measurable utilities, in the *Manuel d'économie politique*: see the 2nd ed. (Paris: Giard, 1927), pp. 617–18. A useful brief survey of the state of welfare economics following the adoption of the Pareto criterion can be found in Melvin W. Reder, *Studies in the Theory of Welfare Economics* (New York: Columbia University Press, 1947). There are later, more sophisticated books, like J. de V. Graaff's *Theoretical Welfare Economics* (Cambridge: Cambridge University Press, 1957) but these are less accessible to readers without advanced training in economics; even Reder's book requires some patience with graphical presentation. I. M. D. Little, *A Critique of Welfare Economics*, 2nd ed. (Oxford: The Clarendon Press, 1957), may also be recommended, with cautions about some of his ventures into philosophical argument, interesting though these are.

In the United States, *laissez-faire* ideas still flourish, even among people who cannot bear to put them into practice; hence, at least in the United States, John Maynard Keynes' essay, *The End of Laissez-Faire* (London, 1926), is still topical, and on *laissez-faire* as an ideology, prophetic rather than retrospective. It is instructive reading anyway. The magical attractions of the theory of the free market and the principle of *laissez-faire*, unmistakably prominent in standard histories of economic thought, can still be easily discerned in the treatment of competitive markets offered by current introductory textbooks. The interested

student should read at least some of the writings of leading current champions of the principle, for example,
Milton Friedman's *Capitalism and Freedom* (Chicago: University of Chicago Press, 1962). The first chapter, on "The
Relation between Economic Freedom and Political Freedom," seems to me palpably fallacious, but the rest of
the book demonstrates the continuing power of the *laissez-
faire* principle to stimulate new ideas about policies. In
Politics, Economics, and Welfare (New York: Harper &
Row, 1953), Robert A. Dahl and Charles E. Lindblom
pay their respects to the attractions of the market and
balance them against the advantages of other processes
for promoting welfare. The influence of their book runs
throughout the latter two parts of the present one.

The account that I give of the census-notion originates
in my doctoral thesis for Cornell (1953) and in the
extended treatment offered of the same subject in the book
that I wrote together with Lindblom, *A Strategy of
Decision: Policy Evaluation as a Social Process* (New
York: The Free Press, 1963). In that book, the reader will
also find a full discussion of the significance of the census-
notion as one means combined with others of restoring
the discredited intelligibility of utilitarianism. The simplifi-
cation achieved by presenting a two-place census was an
idea that Lindblom urged upon me in the course of
writing our joint book. I had been inclined to work
chiefly with a three-place census, since the census was
originally conceived of as a census of happiness, and it
was natural to leave a place open for people who would
be classified as neither happy nor unhappy. (I called it
a "felicific census," the counterpart to the "felicific calculus." The late J. L. Austin, who encouraged me very
much by liking the idea, pointed out that in most of the
examples I offered him the comparison did not involve
specific policies whose effects were to be discovered.
They involved instead comparisons of the condition of

two groups without linking the condition to policies; in those examples, he held, the census should have been called a "felicity census," not a "felicific" one.) It is, of course, possible to have comparative censuses with more than three places; a discussion of this possibility and of the complications that it entrains will be found in *A Strategy of Decision*.

5) For the theory of collective preference, one must again look to economists; for this is the subject that they have been developing under the wholly misleading title of "welfare economics." Kenneth J. Arrow's *Social Choice and Individual Values* (New York: John Wiley & Sons, 1951, 2nd ed., 1963) makes the connection with politics and the theory of voting inescapable. *The Theory of Committees and Elections* (Cambridge: Cambridge University Press, 1958), by Duncan Black, an economist frankly investigating voting rather than welfare economics, contains not only important original contributions but also a fascinating history of the obscure development of the subject. For a penetrating review of current literature, one may consult W. H. Riker, "Voting and the Summation of Preferences," *American Political Science Review*, LV (December 1961), 900–11.

In my own discussion of collective preference, I have tried to make an end run around some of the problems discussed in this literature, and give a view of major aspects of the subject that need not (in my opinion) wait to be treated until those problems have been dealt with. Whether my end run has succeeded, of course, cannot be determined without considering the problems; and the literature about them is interesting in its own right. Arrow, for example, shows that no scheme for expressing collective preference can simultaneously satisfy all of a certain set of apparently reasonable conditions (his conditions, not my conditions). I incline to think the fact no scheme whatever can satisfy them all implies that together the conditions are too stringent; hence the fact that the schemes I have considered would fail them does not seem too damaging.

I have drawn on James M. Buchanan and Gordon Tullock, *The Calculus of Consent: Logical Foundations of Constitutional Democracy* (Ann Arbor: University of Michigan Press, 1962), for the point about how easily a suitably distributed minority can win out over a concentrated majority. (I have made less use of Buchanan's and Tullock's book than I expected to, but I regard it as a brilliant illustration of the fertility of simple formal methods and a compendium of arresting perceptions about majority rule especially in the direct mandate form.)

The account in the text of what I have called a contemporary rationale of American government has been drawn chiefly from Pendleton Herring, *The Politics of Democracy* (New York: Holt, Rinehart & Winston, 1940), E. E. Schattschneider, *Party Government* (New York: Holt, Rinehart & Winston, 1942), and David B. Truman, *The Governmental Process* (New York: Alfred A. Knopf, 1951). A similar picture, with extended attention to questions of formal theory, including the question about weighting intensities of preference, may be found in Robert A. Dahl, *A Preface to Democratic Theory* (Chicago: University of Chicago Press, 1956), which makes unforgettably clear how much this rationale signifies for political philosophy, though it was originally developed in the course of improving descriptive political science. The lessons of this school of thinkers for political philosophy have not been widely drawn; but then neither have their lessons for theory construction in empirical political science, though in Anthony Downs' *An Economic Theory of Democracy* (New York: Harper & Row, 1957), as well as in Buchanan's and Tullock's book mentioned earlier, promising allied developments have occurred in formal theory. My tests, direct and indirect, for collective preference descend from Dahl's test for "polyarchy"; they are stricter in some respects than their ancestor, and laxer in others, but they consist of comparable combinations of ideas.

Acknowledgments

Students in two successive years of my P.P.E. seminar at Dalhousie have wrestled with this book at various stages of completion. I am grateful for their efforts and for their help. In discussions apart from courses with Vincent Oldaker, a Dalhousie graduate student in sociology, I came to appreciate how much that is valuable in the life of groups may be continually threatened by the trenchantly individualistic bias of our concept of welfare.

Some of my obligations to scholars have already been mentioned, in the course of setting forth the bibliography. I mentioned there J. L. Austin's encouragement in connection with the census-notion; I might remark here that I have taken from him something that he insisted upon when we discussed the ignorance of voters, namely, the point that ignorant or not they have to be consulted. The late Paul Henle's comment, also made in conversation, that the Bill of Rights was still useful vis-à-vis government, even if inadequate vis-à-vis employers, has stayed in my mind and found its way into the present book.

The contention that it is reasonable to forego looking for perfect tests of collective preference in favor of working out some that would satisfy advocates of democracy, at least temporarily, illustrates "satisficing," the principle that H. A. Simon would substitute for "maximizing": see Simon's *Models of Man* (New York: John Wiley & Sons, 1957). The construction by which I have sought to move (in Part One of the present book) from the right to private property to the right to a livelihood illustrates a principle akin to "satisficing," namely, the principle of incrementalism, which favors making policy by a succession of steps each small enough to be kept under control even with limited information. This principle, as elaborated by C. E. Lindblom, is treated at length in the book, already mentioned, that I wrote with him. I owe the quotation from William Jennings Bryan, and the attribution, to G. C. Field's excellent book, *Political Theory* (London: Methuen, 1956). Ithiel de Sola Pool suggested to me the importance of distinguishing between the fertility of a political system in generating policy proposals and its efficiency in processing proposals once made. I have also derived from him the notion that with modern techniques of simulation, it is practical to generate reliable predictions of election results from a small number of simple demographic characteristics. (I have probably put a great deal more strain on this notion than he would.)

J. H. Aitchison, J. Murray Beck, and K. A. Heard, colleagues in the Dalhousie political science department, read the manuscript and supplied me with valuable comments, for which I thank them. For the same service, I thank also Vere Chappell, the general editor of the series in which this book is to appear, and Annette Baier, whose remarks led to extensive changes in the Prologue. I am grateful to Chandler Davis and Felix Oppenheim for reading and commenting on my exposition of the mandate test in Part Three.

The book contains a part—though only a minor part— of the topics I set out to discuss in a project of some years ago, still unfinished, which was supported in 1962– 63 by a fellowship awarded me by the John Simon Guggenheim Memorial Foundation. (It also might be held to complete an earlier project, which was supported by the Rockefeller Foundation and has borne fruit in a number of my separate papers; in that project I undertook to analyze one by one a number of different concepts used to test policies and governments.)

I did a substantial amount of the next-to-last full draft

of the book, in addition to other work, while I was a visiting research professor of philosophy at the University of Pittsburgh, during the spring trimester 1965, there to take part in the I.B.M.-Carnegie Foundation project on "The Impact of Technological Change on American Values." The explication of the concept of rights was tried out on the members of the Pittsburgh philosophy department and in a lecture at the University of Chicago; I received a barrage of useful and spirited criticism in both cities.

The mandate test received its major dialectical tryout with the Central Ontario Philosophical Group, meeting at York University in October 1966; I am grateful to Alex Michalos, who was the official commentator on the paper I read then, and to several philosophers who took leading parts in the discussion.

I wish to thank Réjane Seamone, and her colleagues Carol Bowes and Patricia Kenna, for steady and efficient work typing a late draft of the books; Mrs. James Stoker and her assistants of the Dalhousie mimeograph service for their cooperation; and Mrs. Jean Reoch and Miss Anne-Marie Pegg of the staff of the University of Toronto philosophy department for help in reproducing the paper read at York. Nicholas Braybrooke and Geoffrey Braybrooke worked very diligently with me assembling copies of the final manuscript and correcting the printers' proofs. I must also thank Iona Youden for help with proofreading and indexing. The Dalhousie University Research and Development Fund for the Humanities and Social Sciences has underwritten some of the expenses of preparing the book for publication. Anne Olin of Random House has minimized the stresses of final production.

Halifax   D. B.
7 February 1968

Index

ABOUT THE AUTHOR

DAVID BRAYBROOKE, Professor of Philosophy and Politics at Dalhousie University in Nova Scotia, was born in New Jersey and educated at Harvard (B.A., 1948) and Cornell (Ph.D., 1953). He also studied at Oxford on an American Council of Learned Societies fellowship, and returned there later for a year on a grant from the Rockefeller Foundation. He held a Guggenheim fellowship in 1962–1963. In 1965 and again in 1966, Professor Braybrooke was Visiting Research Professor of Philosophy at the University of Pittsburgh for the spring trimester; and in 1966–1967, he was Visiting Professor of Philosophy at the University of Toronto.

Professor Braybrooke was co-author with C. E. Lindblom of *A Strategy of Decision: Policy Evaluation as a Social Process*; he has also edited, with an introduction and running commentary, a book on *Philosophical Problems of the Social Sciences*. He has published articles in a number of journals, among them *The Journal of Philosophy*, *Social Research*, *Analysis*, and *The American Philosophical Quarterly;* and has contributed original essays to a number of collections besides *The Encyclopedia of Philosophy*.

A NOTE ON THE TYPE

The text of this book was set on the Linotype in Janson, a recutting made direct from type cast from matrices long thought to have been made by the Dutchman Anton Janson, who was a practicing type founder in Leipzig during the years 1668–1687. However, it has been conclusively demonstrated that these types are actually the work of Nicholas Kis (1650–1702), a Hungarian, who most probably learned his trade from the master Dutch type founder Kirk Voskens. The type is an excellent example of the influential and sturdy Dutch types that prevailed in England up to the time William Caslon developed his own incomparable designs from these Dutch faces.

Composed, printed, and bound by Colonial Press Inc., Clinton, Mass. Typography by Leon Bolognese.